NORTHUMBRIA'S C

NORTHUMBRIA'S GOLDEN AGE

The Kingdom of Northumbria AD 547-735

Peter J. Fairless B.A.

William Sessions Limited
York, England

ISBN 1 85072 138 6

Printed in 10 on 11 point Plantin Typeface
by William Sessions Limited
The Ebor Press, York, England

Contents

Prefatory Note

VARIOUS PUBLICATIONS HAVE APPEARED over the years touching on some aspect or other of the old kingdom of Northumbria. I have, though, often noted the absence of a concise account of people and events from the beginning of the kingdom to the time of Bede. This book represents an attempt to fill the gap. It should be said that the subject matter is more complex than is generally realised particularly since source materials are few and fragmentary and historians do not always agree in their interpretation of them. Nevertheless I hope that the picture presented here will be helpful to anyone interested in the period.

Peter Fairless

Acknowledgements

I WOULD LIKE TO THANK Mr William K. Sessions of The Ebor Press and his staff for all their interest and help in publishing this book. I would also like to express my thanks to Oxford University Press for permission to use a number of passages from *Bede's Ecclesiastical History of the English People*, ed. B. Colgrave and R. A. B. Mynors (1969) and *Alcuin: The Bishops, Kings and Saints of York* ed. P. Godman (1982); to Cambridge University Press for permission to use passages from *The Life of Bishop Wilfrid by Eddius Stephanus* (1927) and *The Earliest Life of Gregory the Great* (1968) both ed. B. Colgrave; to Phillimore and Company Limited for permission to reproduce extracts from *Nennius' British History and the Welsh Annals* (1980) being Volume 8 of *Arthurian Period Sources* ed. John Morris; to Penguin Books Limited for permission to quote Cædmon's hymn from Bede's *A History of the English Church and People* translated by Leo Sherley-Price revised by R. E. Latham (Penguin Classics, revised edition 1968); to Llanerch Press for permission to quote from their reprint of D. S. Boutflower's translation of the *Anonymous Life of Ceolfrith* (1991); to Edinburgh University Press for permission to use a passage from *The Gododdin. The Oldest Scottish Poem* (1969) translated by K. H. Jackson; and to J. M. Dent and Sons for permission to quote an entry from *The Anglo-Saxon Chronicle* (Everyman, second edition 1954) translated by G. N. Garmonsway.

CHAPTER 1

The coming of the English

An entry in the *Anglo-Saxon Chronicle* for the year 547 records the
beginning of the Northumbrian kingdom:

> In this year Ida, from whom sprang the royal race of the Northumbrians,
> succeeded to the kingdom.

To make sense this has to be seen in the wider context of the coming of the
English to Britain in the years following the withdrawal of Roman troops.
The beginnings of Northumbria and other kingdoms were, ultimately, the
result of the failure by the Romans to subdue fully the British Isles. Their
failure gave way to a long period of turbulence involving four groupings —
Britons, Anglo-Saxons (or English), Scots (the late Roman name applied to
the Irish) and Picts (the "Painted Ones", as the Romans called them, who
came from north of the Forth). The outcome was the almost complete
elimination of the culture, including the speech, of Britons from the south
coast to the Forth. How that was effected is little more than conjecture.

With the failure of total Roman conquest Roman Britain suffered various
barbarian raids, the Antonine Wall was abandoned and Hadrian's Wall
breached twice (the second occasion in 367). In 383 Magnus Maximus, who
was probably *Dux Britanniarum* at the time and who, having led an offensive
against the Picts and Scots the previous year, left with a substantial portion
of the British garrison for Gaul where he held the Western Empire until
388. Barbarian raids in Britain did not end in view of the campaigns of the
Vandal General Stilicho, but because the situation was worse on the Continent Stilicho had by 401 begun to withdraw troops from Britain. In 406-7 the
army in Britain elevated in succession Marcus, Gratian and Constantine III —
the last, if not the others, as a result of fear in Britain of inadequate Roman
defence of Gaul. Constantine took troops, which were still part of the Roman
imperial army, from Britain to Gaul and Spain but, as a result of his over-
ambition, he was executed in 411 by Honorius, the western emperor.

Thereafter, Roman Britain effectively became independent of Rome. With continuing problems over Gaul Rome did not have the resources to re-establish garrisons in Britain. Also, Roman administrators were expelled from Britain although the reasons for this are obscure. Honorius told the local councils to make their own arrangements for defence. The Roman administrative system did not break down at first. Saint Germanus of Auxerre visited Britain in 429 and again in 445-7 and the areas visited (whichever they were, for it is only known that he went to Saint Alban's shrine at Verulamium on the first visit) seem to have enjoyed peace apart from one Pictish and Saxon raid.

It is Gildas in *De Excidio (The Ruin of Britain)*, written in the period 535-550, who tells of the coming of the English who revolted against their British hosts, although Gildas' report of the fire and destruction of British towns by the English cannot be substantiated. Bede's account largely mirrors that of Gildas. Bede had access to and drew on Gildas who he regarded as a reliable authority for the earlier chapters of the *Ecclesiastical History*, a work completed in 731 (and revised in 732) and of which some 160 manuscript copies survive.

According to Gildas the Britons, initially under Ambrosius, resisted the English in a series of battles which culminated in the British victory at the battle of Badon Hill, fought between 490 and 516 and which inaugurated an era of peace and prosperity which continued into Gildas' own time. Gildas refers to a *superbus tyrannus*, who Bede correctly or incorrectly identifies as Vortigern, as having been responsible for inviting the English to Britain in 446-7. 'Vortigern', which roughly means 'high chief' and could have been either a title or a personal name, may have been the son-in-law of Magnus Maximus. This *superbus tyrannus* made a decision, together with a council, to follow the Roman policy of settling the English in defence of Britain against the raids of the Picts and Scots. Under the Romans Germanic troops had been stationed in the north of Roman Britain but opinions differ over whether these personnel founded the English settlements in Deira. Bede identifies the newcomers as Saxons, Angles and Jutes and analyses their distribution in Britain. From "the country of the Angles, that is, the land between the kingdoms of the Jutes and the Saxons, which is called *Angulus*", he says, "came the East Angles, the Middle Angles, the Mercians, and all the Northumbrian race (that is, those people who dwell north of the river Humber) as well as the other Anglian tribes". Bede refers to the kingdoms of his day by their peoples: the East Angles, the South Saxons and the West Saxons, for example. In referring to "those people", Bede means there were several races of people of which one was Germanic in origin and that was Anglian, as opposed to Saxon or Jute. The name Northumbria preserves an English folk name which was probably a contraction of a phrase which, in

Bede's words, meant "those people who dwell north of the river Humber". This river was used in the period, as were other natural features, in identifying the boundary line.

However, Gildas' view of a single coming is untenable, conflicting with archaeological evidence, and the post-Badon peace he alludes to cannot be independently supported. Gildas may have been reporting the situation in his own area, somewhere in western Britain, and unaware of what was happening elsewhere, for example in Wessex where the *Anglo-Saxon Chronicle* records a series of battles involving Britons and English up to Gildas' own day and right through the sixth century. Moreover the *Anglo-Saxon Chronicle* does not corroborate Gildas' account of the English or Badon. It gives the picture from the English side and dating is suspect with references to battles derived from battle poems rather than contemporary documentation. The chronology of the coming of the English is the subject of much debate. Nevertheless, their coming has been postulated in terms of a series of events with at least three identifiable comings, one in 428 or 429 attributable to the actions of the *superbus tyrannus*, one in 441-42 for reasons unknown, and another to Kent in 449-50. Some Saxon settlements in Britain coincide with increased Frankish power on the Continent which prevented their settlement in Gaul.

While the state of the British aristocracy during the Roman period is obscure kings began to appear at some stage, whether — as Gildas implies — after the end of Roman rule in Britain to combat the Scottish and Pictish raids, or later as a fragmentation of the government of the *superbus tyrannus*. British kings, according to a source known as the *Historia Brittonum*, participated in the battle of Badon Hill but neither they, nor those mentioned by Gildas by name, were the only kings. The territories or states controlled by these kings tended to be fairly small and their boundaries were fluid. At first the role of kingship developed slowly with kings appointed, or overturned, by war bands with little regard for the concept of legitimate authority. Gildas comments on civil strife, both in the past and in his own day. This strife could take the form of inter-tribal fighting, often raiding for cattle and slaves who provided useful currency (Bede mentions Aidan ransoming people unjustly sold as slaves), reflecting a struggle for economic resources. Evidence of some northern British kingdoms is provided in the account of resistance to Ida given in the *Historia Brittonum* compiled in Gwynedd in 829-30 by an unknown person but attributed to Nennius. The kingdoms include Rheged and Catraeth (most probably Catterick). Another may have been based at Bamburgh before Ida — Din Guaire — with Outigern as its last king. A tombstone from Yarrowkirk to the west of Dere Street commemorates two princes — Nudus and Dumnogenus, sons of Liberalis — belonging to a British and seemingly Christian ruling family in the early sixth century. This British kingdom in the Tweed basin might have been connected with

3

Brynaich or Bernaccia, the forerunner of Anglian Bernicia. There is very little to show how the English kingdoms developed except for Wessex and Northumbria, and even for these the evidence is nothing more than fragmentary.

For its early entries the *Anglo-Saxon Chronicle* made use of Bede. The year 547 for Ida was calculated by Bede from king lists. But the accuracy of 547 depends upon the accuracy of the king lists. Moreover, 547 is an *Anno Domini* year. Dating from the birth of Christ (*Anno Domini* dating) was devised in 525 by a Syrian monk named Dionysius Exiguus but did not reach Britain until after 630. Events before then were dated by alternative means and had to be recalculated to fit the new *Anno Domini* chronology, a practice with which Bede was fully conversant. The *Ecclesiastical History* was the first major work to use *Anno Domini* dating. Errors could arise, for example, when events dated by reference to Christ's death were incorrectly written up in *Anno Domini* years, with a resulting discrepancy of up to 28 years. It is unlikely that *Anno Domini* dating was adopted in Northumbria before the third quarter of the seventh century at the very earliest.

The king lists — genealogical lists of kings and the number of years they reigned — such as those in the *Anglo-Saxon Chronicle* and *Historia Brittonum*, were used to promote the legitimacy of rulers like Ida and provide genealogies back to Woden. Apart from the reference to this particular god, early names in king lists cannot be guaranteed. Further problems arise because the lists were transmitted orally before being written down and can be shown to be internally inconsistent. Thus if the names, for one thing, are unreliable the lengths of the reigns are also open to question.

It was not until the adoption of Christianity that events, including the accession of kings, came to be recorded at the time of occurrence in the margins of Easter tables. In due course the entries were detached from these tables to form annals. Unfortunately entries in Easter tables could also be made retrospectively. Saints are a particularly good example of this practice with births being entered at the same time as their deaths. It could hardly have been known at birth that they were destined for sainthood.

The material about early Northumbria is included in the *Northern British History* section of the *Historia Brittonum*. It was prepared in Mercia in the eighth century and is independent of Bede. In it the events are recorded from a Northumbrian viewpoint. It may be that the events recorded after 627 were derived from contemporary entries in Easter tables but before that date material, too, was transmitted orally. The northern material was processed by British scribes in view of the use of British battle, personal and nicknames. British elements, including battles between Britons and Northumbrian English, were added. However, the sequence of events in Northumbria's formative years presented in this material is confusing. One passage reads:

4

Ida, son of Eobba, held the countries in the north of Britain, that is north of the Humber Sea, and reigned twelve years, and joined Din Guaire to Bernicia, and these two countries became one country namely ... Deira and Bernicia.

The writer has Ida joining Bamburgh to Bernicia, of which he is the first recorded English king, but Ida may not have taken Bamburgh initially, if at all. The writer knew that Bernicia and Deira became joined (Ida is not credited with the unity), also that Bamburgh had become part of Bernicia by about 600, and tried to provide an explanation but in doing so conflated the two processes. There would have been other leaders of English groups besides Ida who did not succeed in founding dynasties and whose names were therefore forgotten.

References to Bernicia and Deira in the entry imply their prior existence as separate entities. These names are Bede's Latinised forms of the English Bernice and Dere. The English took over the tribal names of the existing British inhabitants but the etymology of the original British names is obscure. Deira may have been derived from the British word 'deifr', meaning 'waters', indicating that the English first settled by rivers such as those which flowed into the Humber. Another meaning which has been put forward is 'oak forest'. Bernicia developed from the British or Votadini kingdom of Bernaccia, which could have meant 'land of the mountain passes'. Bernaccia was independent of another Votadini kingdom, that of Gododdin, with its centre at Edinburgh. Under the English it increased in size and became extended southwards to the Tees, which was the probable boundary line between Bernicia and Deira. This boundary seems to have coincided with the southern boundary of the diocese of Hexham which Richard of Hexham mentions in the twelfth century. The Tyne was less likely to be Bernicia's southern boundary because Oswiu gave his daughter Ælfflæd to Hild at Hartlepool and, belonging to the Bernician dynasty, he would hardly have placed his daughter in a Deiran monastery at a time of tension between the two kingdoms. Also, Bede was ordained by the bishop of Hexham; had his monastery been in Deira he would have been ordained by the bishop of York.

Settlers were apparently more numerous in Deira than in Bernicia. For the latter archaeological evidence is limited to only a dozen sites. Apart from the larger ones at Yeavering and Milfield, two cemeteries — Greenbank (Darlington) and Howick Heugh — have revealed six and ten inhumations respectively, but there are only one or two inhumations at each of the remainder. Most cannot be more specifically dated than to within a century, with only two dated back to the late fifth and early sixth centuries. That no cemetery has been fully excavated does not help with dating. In Deira there are more than three times as many sites mostly within the area around the Humber and including the Vale of York and the Yorkshire Wolds. Cemeteries at

Sancton comprising both inhumations and cremations, and around York, with cremation urns apparently in use in the early fifth century, have been used to argue continuity of English settlements from the late Roman period when land had been granted on a controlled basis. However, there is difficulty in explaining why the English did not expand significantly from the settlements originally established for defence until after about 500. Much uncertainty remains over the origins of these English kingdoms. As for Ida himself, he or his predecessors may have been settled around the Tyne on land given at some time to a group of Angles employed by the Britons for defensive purposes. Some historians prefer the view that Ida originated from the Vale of York and assaulted Bamburgh from the sea.

According to the *Historia Brittonum* Bamburgh itself was given by Æthelfrith to his wife Bebba, from whom it acquired its name with its English 'burgh' suffix. This followed the conventional method of explaining the name of a place by identifying it with an individual. Bede follows the same method but goes no further than saying that Bebba was a former queen. Æthelfrith's wife is known to have been Acha, daughter of Ælle of Deira and sister of Edwin. Given that Din Guaire is a British name and the possible centre of a British kingdom, the English probably did no more than take over a pre-existing British site. This sort of situation occurred elsewhere, for example, at Yeavering, where the English occupied the British Ad Gefrin.

Bamburgh was not taken, however, without fierce British resistance. Battles did not involve large forces though and Bamburgh would have been taken with only a small war band. Later accounts in the sources which mention armies and those killed in battle refer to hundreds or greater numbers, but such figures are rooted in poetic conventions. Although exact numbers involved in particular battles cannot be calculated, forces of more than a thousand would have been most unlikely. There is evidence that in the early Anglo-Saxon period a band numbered from 10 to 35 and an army more than that number. A kingdom might be taken by less than 100 men. Evidence of a warband or bodyguard of a king or relative of the king can be found in the *Anglo-Saxon Chronicle* entry for the battle at Degsastan in which the retinue or troop of the Bernician Theodbald would have been recruited, members of the royal family apart, from the nobility.

In the struggle between Britons and English, Ida's opponent, the *Historia Brittonum* seems to say, was the last British king in the area Outigern who was given credit for having "fought bravely against the English". British opposition intensified with an alliance of four other kings: Urien of Rheged and Catraeth, Rhydderch Hen (died 614) of Strathclyde, and Guallauc and Morcant whose places of origin cannot be precisely established. The *Historia Brittonum* records "sometimes the enemy [English], sometimes the Cymry were victorious". Theodric fought against Urien, and the English (led by

Theodric or Hussa) were blockaded by Urien on Lindisfarne in poetic terms "for three days and three nights". The English were ultimately victorious because of dissension among the British resulting in the murder of Urien at "the instigation of Morcant".

In the *Northern British History* section of the *Historia Brittonum* there is a king list giving Ida's apparent successors and the lengths of their reigns: Adda (eight years), Æthelric (four years), Theodric (seven years), Freodwald (six years) and Hussa (seven years). All except Hussa were sons of Ida and the writer observes that Augustine came to Kent during Freodwald's reign, but this cannot be correct. Material appended to the earliest copy of the *Ecclesiastical History*, made between 734 and 737, inserts another king, Glappa, between Ida and Adda. Although the *Historia Brittonum* list suggests a tidy succession, as does a similar list in the *Anglo-Saxon Chronicle*, it is possible, and it is also implied, that some at least of those named were active at the same time. It is arguable that the events mentioned in the *Historia Brittonum* took place over a fairly short period of time rather than the half century span from Ida to Æthelfrith.

In their domination of Northumbria the English formed only a minority of the population. Despite hostility between Britons and English, and although Gildas paints a picture of English revolt, within Bernicia and Deira anglicization was on the whole a gradual and fairly peaceful process. A small English ruling group took control of a predominantly British population. There was no wholesale massacre of Britons. English place names have been used to explain population changes in the period but a large number of such place names alone is not proof of large numbers of English. Although Bede often translates British place names into English, British place names could be retained by the English for some time before being renamed. English administration and colonisation through English speakers resulted in changes of place names from British to English while, simultaneously, new settlements were given original English names. The English language itself may have spread because of British acceptance of English rule and recognition that it was the English who were the dispensers of patronage. A period of bilingualism was involved. Early on kings and others could be bilingual. Oswald, who had been in exile, could speak Irish and acted as interpreter for Aidan. Oswiu, too, was probably bilingual, particularly if his son's (Aldfrith's) mother was of Irish stock. More specifically, however, bilingualism was an effect of the location of English settlements in close proximity to British ones. The increase in English settlements identifiable by place names, and the increased numerical superiority of the English within several generations, might be explained in terms of a population increase in the English upper strata of society against a static population at lower levels.

7

Above all, English superiority of numbers could be achieved through intermarriage by which, early on, some British personal names continued in use (Cædmon is a British name) not to mention a gradual decline in British numbers through plague epidemics.

CHAPTER 2

Æthelfrith and his successors

ONE ACCOUNT OF BRITISH RESISTANCE to the English not mentioned in the *Historia Brittonum* is provided by the poem *Y Gododdin* attributed to Aneirin. *Y Gododdin* is an elegy on those killed in battle and not an historical record. However, if it does have a basis in fact it provides evidence of an abortive, last ditch attempt to curb growing English power. The poem tells of Mynyddog "Mwynfawr" ("the wealthy") of the Votadini kingdom of Guotodin or Gododdin whose capital was Din Eidyn (Edinburgh) who sent warriors mostly from Gododdin but also from other parts of Britain on a carefully prepared campaign to combat the "heathen" English of Bernicia and Deira. The warriors who were not led by Mynyddog in person were massacred at Catraeth, one of the centres of Northumbrian administration previously controlled by Urien and a Roman site on the northern road system. In the two surviving texts the British force amounted to 300 or 313 men but:

> out of three hundred champions who hastened to Catraeth, alas, none came back but for one man.

It is conceivable that the men belonged to the upper strata of society and had with them their followers so the precise size of the army is open to debate. The poem implies the battle took place before the conversions to Christianity of 627, before Elmet was annexed by Edwin, that Urien was dead and Bernicia did not have the power displayed in 603 when Æthelfrith was victorious at Degsastan. A possible date for the battle is 600 or shortly before which puts it in Æthelfrith's reign.

Æthelfrith
Æthelfrith, son of Æthelric, son of Ida consolidated Bernician and English domination of Deira and under him Northumbria became the principal power in northern Britain. His policies and those of his successors up to and

9

including Ecgfrith were expansionist, eliminating British opposition and dominating other English kingdoms. He was nicknamed the "Artful" or "Twister" according to the *Historia Brittonum*; according to Bede he was "a very brave king and most eager for glory". Of Æthelfrith's treatment of the Britons Bede comments that he

> ravaged the Britons more extensively than any other English ruler and no king had subjected more land to the English race or settled it, having first either exterminated or conquered the natives.

Bede says that even in his own day the Britons in the main had a national hatred for the English.

The *Anglo-Saxon Chronicle* gives the date of Æthelfrith's accession as 593 although this is not certain if Ida was active later than 547. His wife was the daughter of Ælle, king of Deira. Nothing is recorded of Ælle except his name (which is the subject of the pun on "Alleluia" attributed to Gregory the Great). On Ælle's death Æthelfrith annexed Deira and sought unsuccessfully to eliminate Ælle's son Edwin. The *Anglo-Saxon Chronicle* records Ælle's death as being in 584 but this is suspect. It also indicates that Æthelric, Æthelfrith's predecessor was king of Deira but the union of the two kingdoms so early on is unlikely.

Aedan mac Gabran, the Irish king of Dalriada challenged Æthelfrith but was disastrously defeated at Degsastan identified, though not conclusively, with Dawston in Liddesdale in 603. At the battle, according to the *Anglo-Saxon Chronicle* Æthelfrith's brother Theodbald was killed with all his retinue. The *Chronicle* also records that Hering son of Hussa led, or was one of the leaders of, the battle. Another source records that Aedan's son Domingart was also killed but Aedan who was an old man was not present. Aedan lived until 609 apparently having earlier given up his kingdom and entered a monastery. Æthelfrith's victory prevented his enemy's domination of the Scottish lowlands and gave the English supremacy to the Firth of Forth.

After Degsastan Æthelfrith attacked Powys at Chester. The battle was possibly fought in 605 although it could have been as late as 616; Bede dates it "some while" after the conference at Augustine's Oak of 603. The purpose of Æthelfrith's attack whether to prevent alliances between British kingdoms or in some other sense strategic is not clear but it should still be considered in the context of the continuing struggle between English Northumbria and the Britons. Bede's account of the battle is not strictly historical with Æthelfrith presented as an agent of divine retribution. This approach fits in with the tone of the *Ecclesiastical History*, a homily and type of hagiography in which Bede regarded the English as chosen people beginning a new era in the same way as Saint Paul regarded the people of Israel:

Æthelfrith, whom we have already spoken of, collected a great army against the city of legions which is called *Legacæstir* by the English and more correctly *Caerlegion* (Chester) by the Britons, and made a great slaughter of that nation of heretics. When he was about to give battle and saw their priests, who had assembled to pray to God on behalf of the soldiers taking part in the fight, standing apart in a safer place, he asked who they were and for what purpose they had gathered there. Most of them were from the monastery of Bangor, where there was said to be so great a number of monks that, when it was divided into seven parts with superiors over each, no division had less than 300 men, all of whom were accustomed to live by the labour of their hands. After a three days' fast, most of these had come to the battle in order to pray with the others. They had a guard named Brocmail, whose duty it was to protect them against the barbarians' swords while they were praying. When Æthelfrith heard why they had come he said, 'If they are praying to their God against us, then, even if they do not bear arms, they are fighting against us, assailing us as they do with prayers for our defeat'. So he ordered them to be attacked first and then he destroyed the remainder of their wicked host, though not without heavy losses. It is said that in this battle about twelve hundred men were slain who had come to pray and only fifty escaped by flight. Brocmail and his men at the first enemy attack turned their backs on those whom they should have defended, leaving them unarmed and helpless before the swords of their foes. Thus the prophecy of the holy Bishop Augustine was fulfilled, although he had long been translated to the heavenly kingdom, namely that those heretics would also suffer the vengeance of temporal death because they had despised the offer of everlasting salvation.

This battle and many others involved considerable mobility of forces either on the part of the Northumbrians or their opponents. For example, Aedan, Cadwallon and Oswald were defeated at Degsastan, Denisesburn and Oswestry respectively while Æthelfrith and Penda were victorious at Chester and Hatfield Chase. It is not certain whether cavalry was used but it is likely that Edwin like Ecgfrith later had a sea-going force. The motives for particular battles are not always discernible. Battles could be fought for personal glory or loot as well as domination over the British or other English kingdoms. Retaliation for an assassination attempt was undoubtedly the motive for Edwin's attack on the West Saxons. Jealousy or fear of increasing Northumbrian power triggered the pre-emptive strike by Rædwald against Æthelfrith who did not have time to get his whole army together by the river Idle in 616 when Æthelfrith was killed. Æthelfrith's sons went into exile. Rædwald was bretwalda or overlord south of the Humber and the battle was the first known engagement between a king with supremacy south of the

Humber and a king of Northumbria. By 616 the Britons of Wales had been isolated from the Britons of Cumbria and the Northumbrians had extended their power to the Irish sea.

Edwin

Bede says that while in exile during Æthelfrith's reign Edwin "wandered secretly as a fugutive for many years through many places and kingdoms". Although information is sketchy Edwin is known to have stayed at the courts of three kings. A Welsh poem suggests that at one point Edwin had been hosted by Gwynedd.

Edwin spent some time in Mercia although nothing is known about this except that this period of his life is linked to his marriage to Cwenburh daughter of Ceorl king of the Mercians. The marriage produced two sons Osfrith and Eadfrith. Osfrith had a son Yffi. The date of Cwenburh's death is not known.

Immediately before his accession Edwin was at the court of Rædwald. Bede says that while at the court of the East Angles Æthelfrith "sent messengers offering Rædwald large sums of money" to murder Edwin. Rædwald resisted and his defeat of Æthelfrith enabled Edwin to become king of a united Northumbria.

Sometime between 619 and 625 Edwin married Æthelburh having sent an embassy to her brother Eadbald who had succeeded his father Æthelberht as king of Kent in 616. Possibly Edwin had previously visited Kent. Alliances were formed or cemented by marriages. The same applied to Edwin's marriage which had little to do with religion. Through this marriage to the daughter of Æthelberht and his queen Bertha of Paris Edwin created links with the Merovingian court. Æthelburh produced a son and daughter Uscfrea and Eanflæd who survived and a son and daughter Æthelhun and Æthelthryth who died in infancy.

In 626 Cwichelm king of the West Saxons was responsible for an unsuccessful assassination attempt on Edwin. Bede tells how Cwichelm's agent Eomer arrived on Easter Day at the royal residence by the Derwent and tried to stab Edwin with a poisoned dagger but "Lilla, a most devoted thegn ... interposed his own body to receive the blow". Eomer succeeded in killing another of Edwin's men Forthhere and wounded Edwin in the scuffle. Eanflæd was born that same night. Whatever the reason behind the attempt Edwin responded by attacking the West Saxons slaying many including five kings.

Bede observes that Edwin "ruled over all the inhabitants of Britain, English and Britons alike, except for Kent only", an achievement unmatched by any previous English King. The British kingdoms of Rheged and Gododdin and the Irish kingdom of Dalriada were possibly tributaries. At some point Edwin annexed the small British kingdom of Elmet which had until then managed to remain independent and killed its king Ceretic. This act can be viewed as revenge for the murder by poisoning of Edwin's nephew and Ælle's grandson Hereric who was in exile during Æthelfrith's reign with his wife Breguswith at Ceretic's court where Hereric's children Hereswith and Hild were probably born. Hild may have been born after Hereric's death and although Bede does not say so Breguswith probably returned from exile after Æthelfrith's death. The location and existence of Elmet (for as long as it remained independent) may have had the effect of keeping the English north and south of the Humber apart thereby preventing the Northumbrians from entering into early alliances with the kingdoms in the south. Prior to Edwin the bretwaldas only held sway south of the Humber, a significant political border. Bede records that a distinction was maintained for two hundred years between the people north and south of the Humber. Such a distinction was not the whim of Bede but was currency from at least 672 when the "Northumbrian race" were referred to in the record of a synod which met at Hertford in that year.

Edwin took the Isle of Man and attacked North Wales and Anglesey where he besieged Cadwallon. Cadwallon's response was to attack Northumbria in an alliance with Penda. Edwin was slain at Meicen on 12 October 633 after a reign of seventeen years at the age of forty-eight having been a Christian for the last six years of his life. One son Osfrith was also killed and the other Eadfrith submitted but was killed by Penda. There may have been one battle or two. Possibly there was a battle at Meicen followed by a retreat then defeat at Hatfield Chase near Doncaster. Edwin's head was placed in St Peter's Church, York. Æthelburh fled to Kent by sea with Eanflæd, Uscfrea and Yffi accompanied by Paulinus and one of Edwin's men Bass. At the same time Breguswith seems to have gone for safety to the East Angles where her daughter Hereswith had married an unnamed king of that people and produced a son Ealdwulf.

Edwin's defeat virtually saw the end of his own line in Deira. On returning to Kent Æthelburh founded the convent at Lyminge of which she was abbess until her death in 647. Uscfrea and Yffi died in infancy not long after having been sent from Kent to the court of Æthelburh's relative the Frankish king Dagobert I for fear that Oswald would kill them. Edwin's cousin Osric was killed a year later and Osric's son Oswine in 651 which left Eanflæd who was to marry Oswald's brother Oswiu the only survivor.

After Hatfield, the first of three conflicts in which the Welsh allied with Mercia fought Northumbria, Cadwallon and Penda proceeded to devastate Northumbria. Yeavering was burned. Royal courts were peripatetic and Yeavering was one of several places at which Edwin held court; Bede mentions two other, Campodonum near Dewsbury and an unspecified place by the river Derwent where the assassination attempt of 626 occurred. Yeavering had a great hall originating from the fifth century which continued in use intermittently until 685 when it seems to have been abandoned in favour of Mælmin or Milfield. The palace complex at Yeavering was destroyed by fire in 633 but rebuilt by Oswald before being destroyed again at Oswald's death. Campodonum was also burned and later kings held court somewhere in the vicinity of Leeds instead.

The alliance between the Christian British ruler of Gwynedd and the pagan Anglian king of Mercia was an unlikely one but the battle of Hatfield constituted a rebellion fuelled by common resentment of growing Northumbrian power and Edwin's claim to supremacy in particular. Cadwallon may also have regarded Edwin as disloyal in view of the hospitality extended to Edwin during his exile. Edwin was the first of the Northumbrian bretwaldas. The title means "ruler of Britain" and was an informal one involving a relationship akin to that of overlord with under or sub-kings such as those whom Edwin slayed when attacking the West Saxons. Authority was not hereditary but depended on individual ability to achieve and maintain it with military strength. Edwin was the fifth bretwalda, his predecessors being Ælle of the South Saxons, then half a century later Ceawlin of the West Saxons, Æthelberht of Kent and Rædwald of the East Angles. Edwin's successors were the Northumbrians Oswald and Oswiu and, but not explicitly stated as bretwaldas, the Mercians Wulfhere, Æthelbald and Offa. Control by the first four was limited to the south of the Humber whereas the three Northumbrians ruled British and English kingdoms except for Kent. No doubt Edwin was influenced by Roman models and attempted to recreate the old Roman diocese of Britannia for Bede mentions that Edwin had his standard known to the Romans as a "tufa" carried before him (he may have seen one at Rædwald's court). The concept of the bretwalda was important in paving the way for an eventual unified kingdom of England. The emergence of Penda, however, prevented any real form of a united England under Northumbria.

Bede assessed Edwin's reign in terms akin to a golden era:

> there was so great a peace in Britain, wherever the dominion of King Edwin reaches, that as the proverb still runs, a woman with a new-born child could walk throughout the island from sea to sea and take no harm

and

> ... in various places where he had noticed clear springs near the highway, he caused stakes to be set up and bronze drinking cups to be hung on them for the refreshment of travellers.

Bede adds

> No one dared lay hands on them except for their proper purpose

because of the awe in which Edwin was held. By this comment Bede provides a clue to Edwin's personality. Edwin was an ambitious and much travelled man influenced by his experiences in exile, perhaps not altogether to be trusted and a warrior king in the mould of Æthelfrith. He was a man greatly feared.

Oswald

In 633 after Edwin's defeat Northumbria split into its component kingdoms. Eanfrith, eldest son of Æthelfrith who had returned with his brothers Oswald and Oswiu and sister Æbbe from exile among the Picts or Irish, ruled Bernicia. There is evidence to suggest that in exile Eanfrith married a Pictish princess and had a son called Talorcan who became a Pictish king in 653 and who died in 657. Eanfrith also had a daughter who married a king of Strathclyde and whose son was Bruide mac Bile. Osric, son of Edwin's uncle Ælfric (Ælle's brother) ruled Deira. Bede records the agreement of those who who compiled king lists to expunge the names of these two kings because of the devastation of Northumbria and their reversion to heathenism after the departure of Paulinus. They could not withstand the alliance of Cadwallon and Penda and survived no more than a few months. According to Bede "in the following summer [Cadwallon] killed Osric, who had rashly besieged him in a fortified town [possibly York]; he broke out suddenly with all his forces, took Osric by surprise, and destroyed him and all his army". Then "[Cadwallon] occupied the Northumbrian kingdoms ... for a whole year ... ravaging them like a savage tyrant, tearing them to pieces with fearful bloodshed. Finally when Eanfrith came to him unadvisedly to make peace, accompanied only by twelve chosen thegns, he destroyed him as well". The Irish annals say Eanfrith was beheaded.

By 634 Oswald, called "Whiteblade" in the *Historia Brittonum*, had succeeded Eanfrith in Bernicia. Bede records, Oswald "came with an army small in numbers ... and destroyed the abominable leader of the Britons together with the immense force which he boasted was irresistable at ... Denisesburn". Bede's account of this battle at Heavenfield near Hexham falls into the realms of hagiography. Nevertheless, with Cadwallon's defeat in 634 any hopes of a British resurgence under the leadership of Gwynnedd were extinguished.

It has been suggested that Oswald took Edinburgh in 638. This is based on an entry in the Irish annals which refers to the "siege of Etain". Presumably Etain was Edinburgh but the identification cannot be certain. The Northumbrian chronicles do not record a retaliatory invasion of Northumbria at this time when its king, Oswald, was a friend of the Irish and Aidan was active. It cannot be assumed that the besieger was Oswald. Conflict is absent from the sources for the remainder of Oswald's reign, indicative perhaps of the measure of his authority and control. His marriage to Cyneburh daughter of Cynegisl king of Wessex was part of the process of establishing his supremacy south of the Humber. Bede notes Oswald's diplomatic ability not just his prowess as a warrior. Under Oswald

> the kingdoms of Deira and Bernicia which had up to this time been at strife with one another, were peacefully united and became one people.

Oswald had a claim to Deira since he was Edwin's nephew and his mother Acha was Edwin's sister.

Oswald fell at Maserfelth (probably Oswestry) against Penda, as had Edwin, on 5 August 642 aged thirty-eight having reigned for eight years. His remains were dispersed with his head at Lindisfarne, hands and arms at Bamburgh and the remainder at Bardney in Lindsey. Bede does not give the reasons for the battle although it was set in the context of Mercia's attempt to block Northumbrian power. Christianity was not an issue. Bede describes Oswald in terms of his ideal of a warrior king as "humble, kindly and generous to the poor and strangers" but there is a suggestion in the *Ecclesiastical History* in the initial refusal of Bardney monastery to accept Oswald's relics (transferred there by his niece, Oswiu's daughter and wife of Æthelred of Mercia, Osthryth) that Oswald as overlord was disliked. It has to be remembered that Oswald despite his part in the reintroduction of Christianity in Northumbria was a man of his age. The Northumbrian kings have been described as violent and vicious and Oswald cannot be regarded as an exception. After his death his queen, some historians think, was removed from the political scene, pressurised into taking the veil by Osthryth.

Oswiu

On Oswald's death Northumbria split again with his brother Oswiu aged thirty succeeding in Bernicia and Osric's son Oswine who had gone to the West Saxons after his father's death succeeding in Deira. Bede describes Oswiu's twenty-eight year reign as 'troubled'. In or soon after 642 Oswiu married Eanflæd who as a teenager had returned from Kent by sea for the marriage. As Eanflæd was Edwin's daughter Oswiu had a dynastic claim on Deira. Seeking control of both kingdoms Oswiu invaded Deira in 651 and had Oswine murdered on 20 August. According to Bede, one of whose sources was probably Ceolfrith who had been at Gilling monastery, Oswine in the face of a superior armed force disbanded and accompanied by a trusted soldier named Tondhere sought refuge at the house of a nobleman Hunwold whom Oswine thought loyal. Hunwold betrayed them and they were murdered at Gilling, North Yorkshire. Simeon of Durham preserves a late tradition that Oswine was buried at Tynemouth. If this is correct it may have been that Oswiu wanted him buried on Bernician not Deiran territory to prevent the promotion of a cult. Bede in his only description of a Northumbrian king says he was lofty and handsome in appearance, of pleasant speech and courteous in manner, a man more in the mould of the saintly Aidan than a warrior. The glowing terms in which Bede spoke of Edwin and Oswald were not used of their successor Oswiu and his murder of Oswine was probably a prime reason. Northumbria was reunited with Bernicia remaining the stronger partner but with dynastic rivalries and Deira's separatist aspirations continuing for some time.

Oswiu had problems with Mercia, his son Alhfrith from an earlier marriage possibly to Riemmelth, grand-daughter of Rhun map Urbgen, and Oswald's son Æthelwold whom Oswald presumably intended would succeed him as king of Northumbria. After Oswine's murder Deira chose Æthelwold as king. Æthelwold obtained the protection of Mercia for the next three years. Oswiu evidently suffered a number of raids by Penda who besieged and burned Bamburgh during one of them. Motivated by personal hostility Penda sought Oswiu's removal and, according to Nennius and Bede, accompanied by a number of leaders including the British Cadfan of Gwynedd and Æthelhere of the East Angles besieged Oswiu at Iudeu, believed to be Stirling. Although the sequence of events cannot adequately be constructed Oswiu tried to buy Penda off with treasure but the ploy failed. Oswiu with a small army against the large combined forces against him but helped by heavy rain falls which resulted in the river, which probably drained into the Humber, bursting its banks defeated Penda at Winwæd somewhere near Leeds on 15 November 655. Æthelhere was also killed and Cadfan fled. Æthelwold of whom nothing more is heard remained neutral in the battle and survived (Oswiu's younger son Ecgfrith was a hostage at the Mercian court at the time). Oswiu partitioned Mercia. The land south of the Trent was given to Penda's son Peada who had in 653 married Alhflæd Oswiu's daughter by a previous marriage (Alhfrith, Alhflæd's brother, was married to Cyneburh Peada's sister). That part of Mercia north of the Trent was annexed to Northumbria. Peada was murdered in 656 and it is said that Alhflæd was involved, perhaps as Oswiu consolidated control of all Mercia after Penda's defeat. Peada's murder could conceivably have produced, in turn, a feud in which Osthyth was murdered in 697. With Mercia under Northumbrian rule Oswiu achieved overlordship south of the Humber until three Mercian nobles brought Wulfhere Penda's son out of hiding as king. The sources are a virtual blank for Oswiu and Alhfrith after 664 the year of the Synod of Whitby. It is feasible that Alhfrith rebelled against Oswiu and was banished, or more likely, killed. There is nothing to indicate that he had any children. Oswiu died of unspecified but natural causes at the age of fifty-eight on 15 February 670. He was succeeded by his twenty-five year old son Ecgfrith.

Ecgfrith

After Oswiu no Northumbrian king held power to the same extent. Seen against his predecessors Ecgfrith produced no more than a flicker of their achievements. He temporarily regained control of Mercia in 674 after an abortive attack on Northumbria by Wulhere. Eddius mentions that Ecgfrith used a troop of horsemen, the first reference to the use of cavalry by the English. Lindsey previously attached to Mercia was annexed to Northumbria until retaken (the seventh change between the two sides) by Mercia in 679 when Ecgfrith was defeated by Wulfhere's brother and successor Æthelred by the River Trent. (Æthelred later abdicated and entered Bardney monastery). In the battle Ecgfrith's brother Ælfwine, aged eighteen and said by Eddius to be (sub) king of Deira was killed. Peace between the two kingdoms was negotiated with Archbishop Theodore as intermediary although it is not clear whether Theodore became involved by invitation or on his own initiative.

With aspirations south of the Humber terminated Ecgfrith redirected his attention northwards to the Picts and to the Irish. In 684 according to Bede Ecgfrith "sent an army to Ireland under Berht, who wretchedly devastated a harmless race". The purpose of the attack may have been to discourage the Irish in northern Britain from any aggression. Berht is recorded as having been killed in a battle against the Picts in 698. Berht was an ealdorman and in Irish sources he is referred to as the son of Beornhæth. This battle is a rare indication of conflict during Aldfrith's reign.

Then in 685 Ecgfrith having previously with Beornhæth, whose status may have been almost that of an under-king responsible for Northumbrian defences against the Picts, devastated the Picts (Eddius says two rivers, possibly the Avon and Carron, were full of Pictish corpses) attacked the Picts again. The campaign may have been due to a dynastic claim or quarrel against his relative Brude mac Bile. Ecgfrith acted against the advice of his counsellors including Cuthbert and in Bede's account the enemy pretended to retreat and lured Ecgfrith into an ambush. He was killed at Nechtansmere (Dunnichen Moss, Forfar) on 20 May aged forty. In consequence the Northumbrian border lacked security. Another Northumbrian ealdorman Berhtfrith defeated a Pictish army in central Scotland in 711 and thwarted any southward Pictish advance. By 731 the English and Picts enjoyed peace presumably having reached agreement over their boundaries.

Aldfrith

Aldfrith inherited a Northumbria reduced somewhat in size and power. Nevertheless Bede commented that he "ably restored the shattered state of the kingdom" and, as an unnamed monk from Lindisfarne noted, provided peace and stability which together with the king's patronage enabled Northumbrian monasteries and their learning to flourish.

It was doubtful whether Aldfrith would succeed. He was illegitimate, said to be Oswiu's son by Fína an Irish princess (Irish sources say his maternal grandfather was the high king Colman) and half brother to Ecgfrith who had no sons to succeed him. There was probably a power struggle between the different branches of the Bernician family over the succession with the strongest, Oswiu's side, backing Aldfrith. That the succession had been secured in a direct line from Æthelfrith must have involved remarkable and fierce control. Aldfrith had been prepared for the priesthood at Malmesbury where he became friendly with Aldhelm. Aldfrith spent a number of years in exile in Ireland where he was known as a writer of Irish verse although none has survived and was called Fland Fína "blood of wine" a reference to his royal parentage. The anonymous *Life of Cuthbert* implies Aldfrith's presence in Iona the year before he became king but his whereabouts at the time of Ecgfrith's campaign of 685 are not known. After his accession Aldhelm sent him treatises on the mystical significance of the number seven in scripture and the metric art with one hundred riddles he had composed and dedicated to Aldfrith. Aldfrith gave lands to Wearmouth monastery in return for a book on cosmography which Biscop bought at Rome. Adomnan of Iona during a visit to Northumbria presented him with a copy of his book *On the Holy Places* which he had copied and circulated for the benefit of lesser folk. Bede reproduced some extracts in the *Ecclesiastical History*. Bede and Eddius pay tribute to Aldfrith's scholarship as does Alcuin of York who speaks of him as "a scholar with great power of eloquence, of piercing intellect: a king and a teacher at the same time". In his combination of scholarship and warrior skills Aldfrith has been likened to Alfred the Great. He died of unknown natural causes at Driffield on 14 December 705. After his death his wife Cuthburh sister of Ine king of the West Saxons became a nun at Barking and she is believed to have been involved in the foundation of Wimbourne Monastery in Dorset.

CHAPTER 3

Christianity before the seventh century

EVIDENCE OF CHRISTIANITY IN THE AREA which became Anglian Northumbria is slender, with no clear indication of when it was established. Indeed, it is not known precisely when Christianity was introduced into Roman Britain.

References by Tertullian and Origen suggesting that Christianity had been introduced to Britain by 200 are suspect because they, in all probability, sought to project the idea of a church established at the ends of the Roman world, the boundaries of civilization. The martyrdom of Saint Alban does not help in fixing a date. There were three periods of persecution in Britain, two falling within 250-59 — the persecutions of Decius and Valerian — and one, the Great Persecution of Diocletian, 303-11. Gildas links Alban with Verulamium and puts Alban's martyrdom at the time of Diocletian's persecution but admits the latter is conjecture. Nevertheless, Gildas may have had access to some earlier source materials although from the existing evidence, Britain was not affected by Diocletian's persecution.

An alternative date of 209 which has been suggested for Alban's death is unlikely because if Alban had been martyred then the fact would have been transmitted, ultimately to Rome, not too long afterwards but third century Christian writers do not make any reference to Alban or British Christians. It cannot be denied that Christians were persecuted or martyred in Roman Britain at some time although it is difficult to say when. At best it could be said that Alban's death may have occurred during the persecutions of 250-59. By 311 it was recognised that the Christian religion could not be eliminated in the Roman world and Galerian's limited edict of that year was followed in 313 by the edict of Milan issued under Constantine the Great, which raised the status of Christianity considerably.

The first specific reference to British Christianity was in the records of the proceedings of the Council of Arles, 314. Three British bishops, together with two other persons, are mentioned as attending the Council. One of the bishops was from York. Some established structure — of a British church of some twenty bishops with urban churches — can be suggested in the light of a visit to Britain by Victricius, bishop of Rouen, about 395. The purpose of the visit may have been in his capacity as a metropolitan bishop in Gaul meeting with British bishops to deal with not the Pelagian heresy but with a dispute about metropolitan sees in Britain, which an entry in the *Anglo-Saxon Chronicle* indicates was not resolved until 403. That the church encountered by Victricius was orthodox is apparent in the matter of the Pelagian heresy. Constantius, a monk from Lyons, in his *Life of Germanus* explains that bishops in Gaul had been visited by a British party and told how Pelagian ideas had taken a strong hold in Britain. Germanus was twice sent to combat it.

The Latin language can provide evidence of early British Christianity. While attempts to trace the transmission of the Latin language (and its relation to the vernacular British) have not been wholly successful, the survival of Romano-British place names is a pointer to the existence of Christian communities. For example, Egglescliffe and Eccles (Berwickshire) are derived from the Latin *ecclesia*, meaning a body of Christians, used by the Britons and acquired by the Anglo-Saxons. The writings of Saint Patrick indicate that the Old and New Testaments were known during late Roman Britain and Patrick's biblical quotations, together with those of Gildas, show that the version of the Bible adopted was the 'Old Latin' Bible used in Gaul in the third century.

In *De Excidio* Gildas addresses five British kings who were Christians. The bishops alluded to in general terms by Gildas, as well as Bede's two references in the *Ecclesiastical History*, one to "All the British bishops" in a letter from Pope Gregory to Augustine and reproduced by Bede, and the other to the British bishops who met at Augustine's Oak, suggest continuity of organisation. However, the areas covered by episcopal sees would have been affected by the change from the *civitates* of Roman Britain, with their urban centres where the episcopal seats were located, to the native kingdoms of sub- or post-Roman Britain in which the bishops were tribal.

In pre-Anglian Northumbria archaeological evidence for Christianity south of Hadrian's Wall includes graffiti inscriptions, burials and small objects, notably from York, Catterick and Corbridge. Small objects have to be regarded with caution since they may have been brought in from somewhere else. Hoards are more reliable as intentionally hidden collections.

At York, a tile with a *Chi-Rho* symbol (☧) inscribed during production there similar in design to one found on mid-fourth century coins was found below the nave at the east end of York Minster in 1968. It originally belonged to the

Principia, the Roman administrative building. During excavations at the Roman site at Catterick a sandstone block with an inscribed *Chi-Rho* was found in 1959 which had been used on another part of the site before being reused for the exterior of the cold plunge bath which ceased to be utilized in the early fourth century. Also found at the Catterick Roman site was the base of a glass bottle with the same symbol scratched on it. Silver finds at Corbridge indicate a hoard, to which the 'Corbridge Lanx' belonged, with some Christian associations including the *Chi-Rho* symbol which also figured on a jet ring from Chesters Roman site. The symbol, derived from the first letters of *Christos*, was given significance with the conversion to Christianity of Constantine the Great. It was believed that Constantine had a dream in which he saw the *Chi-Rho* symbol (the cross was not in widespread use as a Christian symbol until around 400). Another Christian motif — the fish — has been found on two objects, a late fourth century strap tag with a fish and palm design from the Roman villa at Beadlam, Yorkshire, and from Corbridge a fragment of imported third century glassware with the fish motif alone.

A stone coffin from York (for a girl Simplicia Florentia) has an inscription of apparently Christian associations. The burial was in gypsum which has preservative properties. Gypsum burials were linked with the belief in an imminent and physical resurrection and so could have Christian connotations but, despite some signs of Christianity in York, there is not sufficient evidence to show that burials there, either singly or in groups, were specifically Christian. Another feature of burials, orientation on an east-west axis, often associated with Christianity was also characteristic of pagan cemeteries. Where such orientation in very early graves occurred the church would not have had any control over organization of cemeteries because of the small number of its adherents.

Unfortunately there are no known remains, either in wood or stone, anywhere in Britain from the Roman period of churches specifically built as such. One other form of archaeological evidence cited for early Christianity is the damage to imagery at Mithraic temples at Carrawburgh, Housesteads and Rudchester, probably early in the fourth century. This was possibly caused by enthusiastic Christians, with or without a military involvement, although other explanations could apply.

The pattern of evidence tends to suggest Christian activity from the early fourth century in towns along the major Roman roads. The shortage of evidence in other parts of the North East may be attributable to little or no settlement in the late or sub-Roman period. Alternatively, the lack of archaeological finds could simply mean that Christianity failed to find a foothold in a strong pagan area. It is also not to be presumed that Christianity was predominately urban.

For Christianity north of Hadrian's Wall some hints are given by Bede in a paragraph about Nynia dovetailed into an account of Columba:

> The southern Picts who live on this side of the mountains had, so it is said, long ago given up the errors of idolatry and received the true faith through the preaching of the Word by that reverend and holy man Bishop Ninian, a Briton who had received orthodox instruction at Rome in the faith and the mysteries of the truth. His episcopal see is celebrated for its church, dedicated to St Martin where his body rests, together with those of many other saints. The see is now under English rule. This place which is in the kingdom of Bernicia is commonly called Whithorn, the White House, because Ninian built a church of stone there, using a method unusual among the Britons.

This passage cannot be taken simply as it stands. Less is known of Nynia than Columba for whom there is Adomnan's *Life*. Nynia is a Briton (his name is British, the familiar Ninian is a Latinized version of it) and his orthodox preaching, the "true faith", is contrasted with that of the Irish Columba. Nynia's training is linked with Rome but perhaps this is more in the sense of the ways of the church of Rome than a physical presence there. Bede does not give any dates for Nynia, probably because he did not have any. However, Bede does date Columba's evangelism among the northern Picts (north of the Antonine Wall) after Iona's foundation in 565 and he notes that Nynia had been active before then.

The tribes who lived north of Hadrian's Wall — to the south west (Galloway), the Novantae; on the east, from the Wall to the Forth, the Votadini — were British and ethnically similar to those south of it, unlike the tribes north of the Antonine Wall. The view that Rome had entered into treaties with the tribes between the walls is questioned nowadays. When Bede wrote, the lands of the Novantae were held by the English as part of Bernicia including the episcopal seat of Whithorn whose incumbent, Bede's contemporary, was Pecthelm. The location of Nynia's shrine is referred to as *Candida Casa* ("the White House, because [Nynia] built a church of stone there") and it was dedicated to Martin (of Tours). It is unlikely that the remains visible today at Whithorn are earlier than the late seventh century. What Bede is talking about may be a tradition of a Roman building of dressed stone which was unusual for the area in which it was built. Excavations at Whithorn revealed cremation graves in a cemetery belonging to a Roman settlement which were succeeded by inhumations (orientated east-west) of the late Roman period, regarded as Christian, and also Anglian and later periods. That a see was held by Nynia suggests a Christian community, originating south of Hadrian's Wall before about 400, already in existence in Galloway, being sufficiently large to acquire its own bishop and far enough away from the nearest episcopal seat at Carlisle. If bishops were based in major Roman towns, particularly provincial capitals such as York, Carlisle is a possible candidate for an episcopal seat.

A tombstone from Whithorn of a Briton with a Roman name, Latinus, with a Christian inscription which translated means "We praise thee Lord", supports an established Christian community there in the fifth century, although other tombstones for bishops Viventius and Mavorius, Florentius and (?)Iustus from Kirkmadrine make it likely that Whithorn was not the only Christian community with an episcopal seat.

Nynia cannot be satisfactorily dated by reference to the dedication to Martin of Tours who died in 397. There was seemingly a dedication to Martin at some time but it cannot be linked with Nynia. There is a reference, in both an eighth century poem and the twelfth century *Life* by Ailred of Rievaulx about Nynia, to a British king, Tudwalus, as a contemporary of his. Someone of that name was active about 530-40 but this was not necessarily the British king. From the limited evidence it is suggested that Nynia can be placed somewhere between 400 and 450 with the appointment of a bishop to Whithorn between 400 and 425 in an area where Christianity existed from the late fourth or early fifth century.

As well as linking Nynia with the British Church in Galloway, Bede alludes to the conversion by Nynia of the southern Picts. Their conversion might have been a tradition transmitted by the Picts themselves or to Bede by Trumwine who had been consecrated bishop of these Picts by Archbishop Theodore at York. The tradition may have been reflected in the name Pecthelm which meant "Leader of the Picts". Bede refers to him as the first bishop of Whithorn consecrated 730-31 the earlier see having at some previous time ceased.

The southern Picts apparently occupied territory to the south of the Antonine Wall as well as to the north of it. Gildas, the incidence of Pictish place names, and finds of tombstones and ornamental silver chains, indicate occupancy by the southern Picts of the land from the Tweed and Forth to the Clyde valley between 400 and 600. The area was subsequently subjugated by the Northumbrian Angles under whom a see was established at Abercorn and held by Trumwine from 681. In 685 the southern Picts shook off Northumbrian rule and Trumwine retired to Whitby. Possibly the southern Picts were converted by Nynia or had a preference for the church of Rome but the circumstances are far from clear.

Reference was made above to Carlisle. There is reason to think that Saint Patrick and his family came from a civilian settlement near Birdoswald, based on an interpretation of such place-name references as are given in his writings. Patrick, like Gildas, is extremely sparing in the use of dates and place names. Nevertheless Patrick, who was a Briton, records that his father, Calpurnius, was both a deacon in the church and the holder of civil office and his grandfather, Potitus, had been a priest. (His mother was apparently called Concessa). A chronological framework contructed from material in Patrick's *Confessio* could put the ordination of his father and grandfather at about 420 and 395 respectively and Patrick's birth at around 415. Patrick's captivity during the Irish raids would then be placed at 430 and his return to his native district and training and ordination as deacon, priest and bishop between around 440-55. This framework would make Patrick and Nynia roughly contemporary as well as provide an indicator of the state of the church in the Carlisle area at the time if Patrick was ordained there.

Although the evidence for Christianity in pre-Anglian Northumbria is scarce before 450, after that date there is effectively silence. Possibly by the end of the fifth century the bishop of York had acquired metropolitan status, a status retained in some way by an urban centre in the north of England from a pre-Anglian Deira into a Christianized Northumbria, but of this there is no certainty. Christianity did not die out in Britain after 450 in view of the advent of monasticism in the third quarter of the fifth century. In pre-Anglian Northumbria, because of the small number of English settlers before the end of the sixth century, insufficient to disrupt British life, Christian continuity is possible. If the British church did survive there is nothing to indicate it tried to bring Christianity to the English. Bede makes a general statement to that effect and there is no suggestion in his writing that the missions of Paulinus and Aidan encountered British Christians. In any case the evidence is not strong enough to allow the presumption that in pre-Anglian Northumbria Christianity was more than a minority religion or that its spread had anything of the same force as that given to it by the English.

CHAPTER 4

The mission of Paulinus

A MONK OF WHITBY WHOSE NAME IS NOT KNOWN tells the famous story as does
Bede of the encounter of Gregory the Great with some Deiran boys in Rome:

> ... before he became Pope, there came to Rome certain people of our
> nation, fair-skinned and light-haired. When he heard of their arrival he
> was eager to see them; being prompted by a fortunate intuition, being
> puzzled by their new and unusual appearance, and, above all, being
> inspired by God, he received them and asked what race they belonged
> to. (Now some say they were beautiful boys, while others say that they
> were curly-haired, handsome youths.) They, answered, "The people we
> belong to are called Angles." "Angels of God," he replied. Then he asked
> further, "What is the name of the king of that people?" They said
> "Ælli," whereupon he said, "Alleluia, God's praise must be heard
> there." Then he asked the name of their own tribe, to which they
> answered, "Deire," and he replied, "They shall flee from the wrath
> of God to the faith."

The two versions were produced independently which suggests the tale was
well known in Northumbria. Bede refers to it as a tradition; there is no known
documentary evidence for it and Gregory does not mention it in his letters.
The Whitby version of it comes from the earliest account of the life of
Gregory (if not the earliest extant piece of Anglo-Saxon literature) written
probably between 704 and 714 during the lifetime of Ælfflæd abbess
of Whitby. Included in the *Life* was traditional material which was almost
certainly handed down in Kent from Paulinus to Eanflæd and then to
Ælfflæd who knew Wilfrid who was himself familiar with Rome. Bede would
have used it had he known about it. Bede also used traditional stories, fewer
than in the Whitby version, but he did have the advantage of copies of letters
written by Gregory and other popes.

There are differences between the two accounts. For example, in the *Ecclesiastical History* Gregory goes to the market place and obtains information from bystanders whereas in the Whitby account the boys were received by Gregory who conversed with them direct regardless of linguistic differences. In Bede the boys are specifically referred to as slaves and the inhabitants of Britain are pagans. The meeting constitutes more than curiosity on Gregory's part for he expresses an interest in slaves in his letter of September 595 to the priest Candidus who was leaving Rome for Gaul where he was to administer papal estates. Candidus was instructed to buy English boys aged about seventeen or eighteen so that they could then be trained in monasteries in Rome. They could then be sent back to England as missionaries or to assist missionaries. There are other similar instances, for example, Bede mentions the slaves freed by Aidan, some of whom were trained by him and the acquisition of thirty Danish boys by Willibrord. Gregory may have first become aware of the English in Britain through his interest in the church of Gaul and the administration of papal estates there and the letter of 595 implies he knew about the pagan English by that time. However, the purchase of English slaves was not the main purpose of the letter which does not specifically refer to a major mission of conversion of the English. This is not to say that Gregory did not have plans for a mission, the attraction of which lay in the recovery, as it were, of a Roman province as part of a concept of a new spiritual Roman Empire at a time when the universal authority of the church of Rome was threatened by the Gallic, Spanish and Irish churches and the growing power of the Lombards in Italy.

Whatever moved Gregory to initiate a mission the story of the Deiran youths was used to express his desire to spread the Christian message. Kent was a suitable base for the mission. As well as being the point of arrival for travellers from the Continent its king Æthelberht was pre-eminent over other English kings and his wife was the Christian Bertha daughter of the Frankish King Charibert. Thus both Gregory and Æthelberht had connections with Gaul through which Augustine and his party would travel. Æthelberht's marriage had taken place by 590 and Bertha had been accompanied to Kent by her Frankish chaplain Liudhard. Christianity had therefore been practised in Æthelberht's court for some years but with apparently no attempt to convert the king. Gregory chose Augustine, prior of Gregory's own monastery of Saint Andrew at Rome, to lead the mission and in so doing was following precedents in using monks for missionary work. The sole evidence for the beginning of the mission is in the *Ecclesiastical History* when Bede dates it to the fourteenth year of the Emperor Maurice. This year ran from August 595 to August 596 and the mission probably began early in 596. After a temporary setback when Augustine returned to Rome seemingly because of doubts within Augustine's party about the mission, Augustine set out again from Rome in or shortly after July 596 having been invested with more authority from Gregory. He landed at Thanet with a group said to have been forty in number in the spring or summer of 597.

The distribution of place names with heathen associations in the south of England emphasises the strength of established heathenism confronting the mission. However, late in 597 or early 598 Augustine sent two members of the mission, the priest Laurence and the monk Peter, back to Rome to report the progress that had been made together with a request for advice from Gregory on various matters. Laurence returned, with or without Peter, in the summer of 601 accompanied apparently among others by the abbot Mellitus and Justus who were subsequently consecrated bishops of London and Rochester respectively and Paulinus.

The Whitby monk did not appreciate there were two missionary groups treating them as one in his *Life* of Gregory. The second party of 601 brought with them a reply from Gregory known as the *Libellus Responsionum*. Although its origins and authenticity have been subject to some debate and the text as reproduced by Bede is corrupt, in it Gregory instructed Augustine to consecrate twelve bishops who would be subject to him. Augustine was to allocate a bishop to York and if Christianity took root in the north the bishop of York would consecrate twelve other bishops and have metropolitan status although all would be subject to Augustine. After Augustine's death York would be independent of Canterbury with each metropolitan receiving the pallium from the pope with their precedence dependent upon seniority of consecration.

The idea behind this was to set up an ecclesiastical organisation reflecting the secular situation in the southern kingdoms with their overlord and an independent Northumbria. This did not materialise. York did not have an archbishop until 735 and then it had only three, not twelve, suffragan bishops at Lindisfarne, Hexham and Whithorn.

Bede's knowledge about Augustine's mission was limited to the information sent by Albinus abbot of the monastery of Saints Peter and Paul, Canterbury and Nothelm, later archbishop of Canterbury, who had visited Rome and researched the papal archives. Bede knew little of Æthelberht's conversion and it is unclear whether he was a Christian by the time of the second mission. Among the letters written by Gregory in 601 was one addressed to Æthelberht which does not explicitly say he was a converted Christian but might have been written on the basis that he was. Whatever the date he must have been baptised before 616 the year of his death. Conversion was not simply a matter of religion to Æthelberht but of the usefulness of the Christian God in winning battles and acquiring wealth. Although aware of Christianity among the Franks Æthelberht may have preferred to accept Christianity from Rome rather than the Franks and so maintain his independence. He may have been prevented from an early acceptance of Christianity because of the entrenched paganism in Kent noted above and the other English kingdoms of which he was overlord. Christianity had to be accepted by his sub-kings otherwise his position as bretwalda would be compromised if they rebelled invoking the aid of their pagan gods. Even when Christianity prevailed in a kingdom there was still probably an anti-Christian faction the existence and strength of which was apparent for instance in Northumbria with the return to paganism after Edwin's death.

The extension of Augustine's mission to northern England was facilitated by the marriage of Edwin to Æthelburh. In Bede's account of this political marriage, when Edwin sent an embassy to Eadbald to arrange the marriage Eadbald (who had during a short period after his accession apostacized) responded that a Christian maiden could not marry a heathen husband. Edwin promised freedom of religious observance to Æthelburh (the date she embraced Christianity is not known) and her household and expressed willingness to accept Christianity subject to a satisfactory examination of it. Aspects of Edwin's conversion are reminiscent of the conversion of Clovis as told by Gregory of Tours. Eadbald agreed to the marriage and Æthelburh travelled north with Paulinus as her chaplain. Paulinus was consecrated bishop on 21 July 625 by Justus. Although Northumbria was pagan Edwin's marriage was not the occasion of his first encounter with Christianity. During his exile at Gwynedd he would have come into contact with the British church. There is a tradition preserved in the *Historia Brittonum* that Edwin was baptised by a British bishop but this is generally rejected. The tradition possibly arose from a British refusal to acknowledge Paulinus' role in the conversion of Northumbria.

After surviving the assassination attempt of 626 Edwin declared that he would accept Christianity if he was successful in war against the West Saxons and had Eanflæd baptized as a pledge. She was duly baptized at Pentecost 626 with twelve others and thus the first baptized Northumbrian Christian. Despite his victory against the West Saxons Edwin would not adopt Christianity without due consideration:

> But first he made it his business, as opportunity occurred, to learn the faith systematically from the venerable Bishop Paulinus, and then to consult with the counsellors whom he considered the wisest, as to what they thought he ought to do. He himself being a man of great natural sagacity would often sit alone for long periods in silence, but in his innermost thoughts he was deliberating with himself as to what he ought to do and which religion he should adhere to.

At some point although it is difficult to say when Edwin and Æthelburh each received a letter from the current pope Boniface V (619-25). The texts are copied in the *Ecclesiastical History* and were probably obtained from Kent rather than Northumbria because of the turmoil following Edwin's death. Boniface holding up the conversion of Eadbald as an example urged Edwin to accept Christianity and sent him a tunic with a golden ornament and a cloak. In the letter to Æthelburh Boniface says she "continuously shines in pious works pleasing to God" and at the same time reminds her of her duty to persevere in working for Edwin's conversion. Boniface sent her a silver mirror and a gold and ivory comb.

Edwin would not accept Christianity until he had held a meeting with his loyal chief men and his counsellors, in effect the Northumbrian Witan, at which Paulinus was present. Before the meeting Paulinus reminded Edwin of an encounter with a stranger while the king was in exile at Rædwald's court. After learning of Æthelfrith's attempt to have him murdered, Edwin sitting outside Rædwald's palace at night received a visit from a stranger who knew about Edwin's predicament. He asked Edwin how he would reward the man who could extricate him and make him a great king. Edwin after replying that he would offer suitable gratitude was asked whether he would promise to obey and accept the saving advice of such a man if he could give the best counsel of all. After Edwin agreed the stranger laid his right hand on Edwin's head and told him to remember the sign and honour his promises when he came across it again. When Edwin was hesitating to accept Christianity Paulinus placed his right hand on his head and enquired if he remembered the sign. The tale is also told by the Whitby monk but whereas he identifies the stanger with Paulinus Bede does not.

Nothing is known about Paulinus' activities between 601 and his journey to Northumbria, a period of between 18 and 24 years. Presumably he was in Kent throughout although the story of the visitor to Edwin at Raedwald's court might represent a tradition that Paulinus visited the East Angles. The connection here would be that Rædwald was baptized in Kent and might have met him there. The story, true or not, reflects Paulinus' awareness of Edwin's situation and appeal to Edwin that it was a higher authority than Rædwald who had allowed him to survive and established him in his kingdom and that God's agent in the matter was Paulinus.

Although Bede records the council meeting verbatim, as he does with the Synod of Whitby, it is improbable that he had access to any surviving records. Dialogue was also used by Gregory of Tours in *The History of Franks* one of Bede's exemplars and here Bede is using it as a vehicle to get his point across. It is the Christian, not the pagan, religion which can explain the mysteries of life and death a message made in probably the most famous passage of Bede's:

This is how the present life of man on earth, King, appears to me in comparison with that time which is unknown to us. You are sitting feasting with your ealdormen and thegns in winter time; the fire is burning on the hearth in the middle of the hall and all inside is warm, while outside the wintry storms of rain and snow are raging; and a sparrow flies swiftly through the hall. It enters in at one door and quickly flies out through the other. For the few moments it is inside, the storm and wintry tempest cannot touch it, but after the briefest moment of calm, it flits from your sight, out of the wintry storm and into it again. So this life of man appears but for a moment; what follows or indeed what went before, we know not at all.

But the chief priest Coifi's motivation for a change of religion is presented as materialistic geared to his personal well-being. The pagan faction did not have any effective argument for its case and Bede was not in any position to give it one. When Edwin finally decided for Christianity Coifi (not Paulinus) was the first to denounce the old religion. On a stallion and armed with a spear, both previously forbidden to a chief priest, Coifi set off to destroy the pagan temple at Goodmanham.

Edwin's delay in accepting Christianity was, like Æthelberht's, due to political considerations in that Rædwald had initially adopted Christianity while an underking visiting Æthelberht in Kent but on returning to his kingdom relapsed (Bede lays the blame on Rædwald's wife). Rædwald's apostasy was possibly a necessary step to becoming a bretwalda himself rejecting Kentish supremacy towards the close of Æthelberht's long reign. With Rædwald as bretwalda it would have been difficult for Edwin to accept Christianity from Kent under a pagan overlord. The circumstances were too similar and Edwin had to wait until a change occurred in the political climate when he was in a strong enough position to convert to Christianity. Once bretwalda himself, Edwin followed the practice of making sure his underkings followed suit and was responsible for the baptism of Rædwald's successor Eorpwold. This explanation of Edwin's delay is given greater plausibility if the chronology provided by Bede is adjusted. According to Bede Paulinus was consecrated bishop of York at the beginning of his Northumbrian mission. If Paulinus accompanied Æthelburh to Northumbria in 619 and Edwin was baptized in 627 then Edwin's conversion would have been delayed for about eight years whereas Bede's chronology telescopes events into two. One objection to an adjusted chronology is that it casts doubt on the dates which were provided by Bede as conceivably transmitted by Hild, Eanflæd and Ælfflæd. The objection though is not altogether valid since Bede could simply have been misinformed.

Edwin was baptized in a ceremony of mass baptism in York on Easter Day, 12 April 627 in a wooden oratory he had built for the purpose. Edwin began to build a stone church dedicated to Saint Peter to enclose the oratory but he died before its completion. Oswald finished it but within thirty years of his death it suffered from considerable neglect. There are no remains of this church which was used as a royal mausoleum and was still standing in about 1080 although precisely where is not known. Edwin and Paulinus in York are mentioned by the Whitby monk having left a meeting at which issues of heathenism and unlawful marriages had been discussed. From the description given the meeting place could have been *Principia* itself which survived through the early Anglo-Saxon period.

Hild aged about thirteen was baptized with Edwin and at times not specified by Bede Osric of Deira and Edwin's offspring were also baptized — Osfrith, Eadfrith and Yffi, and Æthelhun, Æthelthryth and Uscfrea. Æthelhun and Æthelthryth says Bede "were snatched from this life while they were still wearing [their white baptismal robes] and are buried in the church at York". A six year concentrated programme of evangelism followed, previous attempts by Paulinus at conversion in Northumbria having failed. Paulinus taught and baptized in the river Glen for thirty-six days. At Yeavering the sites of a wooden church (perhaps in prior use as a heathen temple) and an amphitheatre probably used by Paulinus have been discovered. Paulinus operated from royal centres such as York and Goodmanham from which he baptized in the Swale near Catterick. At Campodonum Paulinus built a church which was destroyed when Northumbria was devastated in 633-34 although the stone altar survived and was preserved in the monastery of Elmet Wood ruled by Abbot Thrythwulf.

Paulinus' missionary activity extended to Lindsey then part of Northumbria. His first converts were the reeve of Lincoln Blæcca and his family. At Lincoln Paulinus built a stone church, the walls of which were still standing in Bede's day, but either through neglect or enemy damage had lost its roof. This church has tentatively been identified with the earlier phase of the church of Saint Paul in the Bail. In it Paulinus as the only bishop in the English church at the time consecrated Honorius archbishop of Canterbury between 627 and 631. Bede preserves a century old and somewhat stylized description of Paulinus emanating from the Lindsey mission given by an old man to Deda abbot of the monastery at Partney:

> he was tall, with a slight stoop, black hair, a thin face, a slender aquiline nose, and at the same time he was both venerable and awe-inspiring in appearance

The rate of success of Paulinus' mission in Northumbria signalled a second metropolitan see at York and Pope Honorius I wrote in June 634 to Edwin and Archbishop Honorius of Canterbury sending the pallium for Paulinus and making provision that either archbishop would consecrate a successor in the event of the other's death. Unfortunately communications were such that Edwin had been dead and Paulinus back in Kent since October 633. Dependent on Edwin's patronage, with the king dead there was little else that Paulinus could realistically do other than to return to Kent. His flight would not have been favourably regarded by the populace and this together with heathen elements not wholly suppressed contributed to the apostasy abhorred by Bede. Christianity was not totally lost without trace. While Paulinus in Kent was granted the vacant episcopal see of Rochester (which he held until his death on 10 October 644) in Northumbria the deacon James an Italian who had accompanied Paulinus continued the work of the mission without interference. James living in a village near Catterick which Bede could not identify taught and baptized. He was skilled in the Gregorian chant which he taught when peace was restored. He lived through the years of the Irish mission to Northumbria, was present at the Synod of Whitby on the Roman side and died early in Bede's lifetime, probably in the 670s, of considerable age.

CHAPTER 5

Aidan and the Irish mission

OSWALD'S VICTORY OVER CADWALLON described by Bede falls within the realms of hagiography. Of Denisesburn Bede says "no symbol of the Christian faith, no church, and no altar had been erected in the whole of Bernicia before ... [Oswald] ... set up the standard of the holy cross" before giving battle. The cross motif here is reminiscent of the dream before battle of Constantine the Great. This cross may have been the beginning of the cult of the cross in Northumbria which subsequently produced many free-standing stone crosses some of which were memorials to particular people and others may have marked Christian meeting places where masses were celebrated by bishops and priests using portable altars. Bede's comments may have been made in ignorance of earlier wooden structures which had been destroyed before his time although he takes care to qualify his statement by the words "as far as we know". Another feature of the Christian dimension given to Denisesburn is that according to Adomnan's *Life of Columba* written between 688 and 704 and of which Bede may not have been aware, Oswald had a vision of Columba on the eve of battle in which he was promised victory as the result of the saint's intercession. Adomnan says that his predecessor Failbe heard of the vision from Oswald himself.

With Cadwallon's defeat behind him Oswald proceeded to re-establish Christianity in Northumbria. Not surprisingly he sent to the Irish elders for a bishop. Eanfrith, Oswald and Oswiu, the sons of Æthelfrith, and their sister Æbbe had been baptised during their seventeen year period in exile when they had lived peacefully among the Picts and Irish. It has been assumed that Oswald had been baptised at Iona but, while Oswald had probably been a visitor there, neither Bede nor Adomnan categorically say so. Adomnan's *Life* only mentions that Oswald was baptised with twelve men. The *Life* also does not suggest that Adomnan was aware of Paulinus and his work.

Bede comments that the man sent to Northumbria in response to Oswald's

34

request was of austere disposition and was not accepted by the English whom he regarded as obstinate and barbarous. On his return a conference was held at which the monk Aidan expressed the opinion that the man had been too severe on the English and had not followed the precedent of the Apostles by starting with "the milk of simpler teaching" and progressing from there. Aidan, of whose earlier life nothing is known, was consecrated bishop and sent to Northumbria in his place. The year was 635 when Segene was abbot of Iona.

Aidan is described by Bede as "a man of outstanding gentleness, devotion and moderation". Even if the language is conventional there is a sharp contrast between the personalities and methods of the Roman and Irish churches represented by Paulinus and Aidan recorded by Bede, for example, in the mass conversions by Paulinus compared with the steady compassionate approach of Aidan. To some extent at least this is due to the selective nature of the information provided to Bede by Albinus which expresses the importance of the virtue of *gravitas* or dignity advocated in the way of life in the Roman church. But at other times Bede uses Roman qualities in his account of Aidan. His serenity was derived from Gregory the Great.

The new Northumbrian Christian initiative was based at Lindisfarne rather than York because the former's location with its seclusion provided at high tide appealed to the ascetic Aidan. From Lindisfarne Aidan would sail to the Farne Islands as a retreat and the place where he used to sit was known in Bede's day. Bede mentions that Aidan used to retire to pray. Gregory the Great held that prayer was necessary for those engaged in the active life. Aidan's desire for solitude serves as a reminder of the importance to the Irish of nature which revealed the ways of God. A significant aspect of solitude was pilgrimage which for the hermit was a mental, not a physical, journey concentrating on the search for God with, in the body, the abandonment of earthly concerns. Moreover, it was Lindisfarne rather than Canterbury which was to all intents and purposes the English centre of Christianity at this time. This was attributable to the qualities of the Lindisfarne monks and the support of Lindisfarne by the Northumbrian kings as bretwaldas.

Irish Christianity was mainly monastic. Irish and British monasticism developed simultaneously in the sixth century influenced by activity in Gaul where Martin of Tours was one of the earliest to adopt Eastern monasticism. Irish monasticism can be linked to the lack of towns so that in a tribal society abbots, who ruled the monasteries, became more important than the bishops. For bishops spiritual matters became more important than administration. This was demonstrated by a life of humility and subordination to the abbot. Bede regarded Aidan as Lindisfarne's first bishop, probably more of a reflection of the ecclesiastical structure Bede was familiar with than reality. Since Aidan spent most of his time travelling he would most likely have regarded himself as a bishop of the Northumbrians rather than Lindisfarne specifically. Aidan was first a monk and he and the monastery he founded on Lindisfarne conformed to Irish ways. Lindisfarne was only one of a number of such foundations in Northumbria. Bede notes the influx of many Irish after Lindisfarne's foundation:

> Churches were built in various places and the people flocked together with joy to hear the Word. Lands and property of other kinds were given by royal bounty to establish monasteries, and English children, as well as their elders, were instructed by Irish teachers in advanced studies and in the observance of the discipline of a Rule.

Bede sought to hold up Aidan as an example to the clergy of his own time. He also stresses that Aidan did not conform with Rome in the observance of Easter although he acknowledges that Aidan was held in considerable respect inside and outside Northumbria and was not censored for the failure to conform. Bede overcame the difficulty of Aidan's observance of the Irish Easter by registering his objection and assuming the historian's role in providing an accurate account of Aidan's life and commending his virtues.

Aidan and his followers lived as they taught. If wealthy people did wrong he did not remain silent out of fear indicative of the strong personalities of the Irish and Irish-trained missionaries. He had no interest in material things and if he was given money by the wealthy he either distributed it for the needs of the poor or ransomed slaves. Some stories about Aidan are presented in a court setting and while Bede observes that Aidan seldom ate with the king there are nevertheless a number of occasions when he dines in the company of Oswald and Oswine although he ate sparingly. On one occasion at Easter-time while Oswald and Aidan were dining a silver dish with rich food was set before them. However, with a great crowd of needy people outside Oswald ordered his own food to be given to the poor and the silver dish to be broken up and distributed to them. A similar story is told by Gregory of Tours.

Such occasions reflect the likelihood that some of Bede's sources about Aidan were derived from the court, in particular from material primarily intended to present Northumbrian kings in a good light. They also reflect a problem for Aidan in that while engaged on missionary work he relied on the king's patronage and contact with the nobility to do it. He often operated from the king's country seats and Lindisfarne, apart from the seclusion it offered, had a good harbour and was close to the capital at Bamburgh. Furthermore Oswald had to act on a number of occasions as interpreter for him.

Aidan was a personal friend of Oswine. Bede tells how Aidan gave away a choice horse, a present from Oswine. The story emphasises Oswine's humility and shows how Irish churchmen would not always conform to convention. Although Aidan was given the horse so he could ride when crossing rivers or making difficult or urgent journeys he ordinarily travelled on foot. Not only did travel on foot make it easier to communicate with people it also avoided grandiosity at a time when riding a horse reflected social position. The use of a horse for transport had been rejected by Martin of Tours. Aidan foretold Oswine's death. With the prevailing tensions between Bernicia and Deira this is not surprising. Aidan dependent on the support of the Bernician kings would not have been above politics and must have kept a careful balance in his relations between Oswine and Oswiu under whom Aidan retained his office for the last nine years of his episcopate. Oswine's murder serves as a reminder that adherence to Christianity was no guarantee of the exercise of Christian morality.

Eleven days after Oswine's death Aidan died (it has been suggested as the result of a stroke precipitated by Oswine's death) at Bamburgh after a mission of sixteen years. He was buried at Lindisfarne although some of his remains were removed by Colman after the Synod of Whitby.

The miraculous has an important role in Bede's account of Aidan, his first patron Oswald and many others in the *Ecclesiastical History*. Significantly Aidan was the subject of a cult whereas Paulinus was not. Some accounts of miracles originate from Aidan's own monastery at Lindisfarne, others from people whom Bede knew personally and considered respectable and reliable, members of the same educated circle as himself. Miracles were popularly used to explain recoveries at a time of very limited medical knowledge although Bede himself did not discount the possibility of natural causes. Rather he was more concerned with such features of miracle stories as prayer and prophecy and, importantly, moral virtue and spirituality especially in the light of the extent to which they were present in the individuals to whom the miracles were attributed: In turn the attribution of miracles stressed the importance of the individuals in the conversion of the English. Thus the miraculous had a particular purpose, a structural function in Bede's writing.

The miracles attributed to Aidan occurred both during his lifetime and after his death. In the former category is the prophecy, subsequently realised, by Aidan of a storm as the priest Utta (who became abbot of Gateshead) escorted Eanflæd who was to marry Oswiu by sea to Northumbria. In anticipation Aidan gave Utta some oil to pour on the sea to calm it. Bede's source was Cynemund a priest from Jarrow who heard it from Utta.

Another miracle told by those "who were in a position to know" occurred while Penda was ravaging Northumbria. Penda attempted to burn Bamburgh using materials from neighbouring villages at a time when the wind was favourable. Aidan, on one of the Farne Islands praying, saw the fire and smoke. On raising his eyes and hands to heaven declaring "O Lord, see how much evil Penda is doing" the wind direction changed and Penda was foiled. After Aidan's days when Penda made another attempt to destroy Bamburgh by fire a beam in the church founded by Aidan and against which he leaned when he died survived. A new church was built using this beam and it survived yet a third occasion when village and church were set on fire, this time accidently. When the church was rebuilt the beam was set up in it as a reminder of these miracles. Many were subsequently healed at the place or cut chips from the beam and immersed them in water which was drunk as a curative.

All the miracles attributed to Oswald were posthumous occurring once he was regarded as a cult figure, and linked either with his victory over Cadwallon or his death. They nearly all involved healing and were possible Bede says because of Oswald's "great faith in God and his devotion" in life. Bede does not supply any dates for what he records but as with Aidan's miracles relies on good authority.

At the place where Oswald prayed on the eve of battle with Cadwallon many miracles were known to have taken place. Many took splinters from the cross erected by Oswald for immersion in water to heal. The monks at Hexham made pilgrimages to the site on the anniversary of his death and built a church there. On one occasion a Hexham monk Bothelm slipped on the ice at night. Suffering considerable pain he asked another monk who was going to the site the following day to bring back a piece of the cross. At the evening meal Bothelm was given some of the moss from its surface and placed it next to his breast but on retiring forgot to remove it. During the night he awoke feeling something cold at his side and putting in his hand to find out what it was found his arm cured.

From Maserfelth where Oswald was killed fighting "the heathen" dust was taken which like the chips of the Heavenfield cross was put in water and consumed. So much dust was taken that a pit was left in which a man could stand. Not only were people cured but animals as well. Bede tells how not long after Oswald's death a horse which had collapsed on rolling over the spot where Oswald died recovered. The horse's rider thereafter reaching an inn found that the landlord's niece had long been paralysed. The girl was taken in a cart to the same site and after a short sleep awoke cured.

In an account similar to the burning of Bamburgh church a Briton (Oswald's miracles were universal) crossing Maserfelth found a spot particularly green. Recognising it as one where a saintly person had died he took some earth for the purpose of healing. Arriving at a house that night he hung the earth, wrapped in a linen cloth, from the beam of the wall. While eating and drinking sparks from a fire in the centre of the room set fire to the roof. Although the house burned down the beam survived.

Queen Osthryth of Mercia, Oswald's niece, wanted her uncle's remains interred at Bardney monastery where Oswald's cult was developed. As Bede tells it the monks were reluctant to accept the remains and the wagon containing them was left outside. Throughout the night "a column of light stretched from the carriage right up to heaven". The monks regarded this as a special sign and took in the remains which after being washed were laid in a splendid tomb. The water in which the bones were washed was poured over earth in the corner of the monastery cemetery. In consequence the earth was endowed with special qualities and could be used to expel devils from those possessed.

Some time later when Osthryth was staying at Bardney Æthelhild, abbess of a neighbouring monastery, took some dust from the pavement on which water used to wash Oswald's bones had been spilt. A male guest at her monastery who was possessed was cured when the casket containing the dust was brought into his presence. Æthelhild was alive in Bede's day and to endorse her reliability as a witness Bede mentions that she was a sister of Bishop Æthelwine of Lindsey and Abbot Ealdwine of Partney.

Bede tells of two miracles involving boys, one at Oswald's tomb, the other on the anniversary of his death. In the first a little boy at Bardney monastery badly affected by ague was taken before an attack by one of the brothers to sit by Oswald's tomb and thereby permanently cured. Details of the second story were provided by Acca to Bede, Acca having been told it by the monks of Selsey monastery founded by Wilfrid which was stricken during a plague epidemic. A Saxon boy who had recently become a Christian had a vision of certain Apostles (apparently Peter and Paul) who told him not to fear death and that he would be carried to heaven, a favour granted at the intercession of King Oswald. He was also told that no-one else in the monastery would die of plague. Shortly afterwards the boy mentioned this to the priest Eappa. The boy died but no one else did.

Finally, Oswald's miracles extended to sufferers in Germany and Ireland. Acca and Wilfrid were told by Willibrord about miracles in Frisia attributed to Oswald's relics. Willibrord also told them how when he was in Ireland a scholar previously apathetic about his salvation feared hell in the possible face of death during an outbreak of plague. At the man's request a portion of the stake on which Oswald's head had been fixed was immersed in some water and blessed. The man drank it and was cured and adhered to the Christian faith for the rest of his life.

Aidan was succeeded as bishop in 651 by Finan an Irishman sent from Iona. His personality was evidently very different from Aidan's for Bede, in the context of the Easter question, says he was "of fierce temper" whom reproof made more obstinate and hostile to the truth. During Finan's episcopate Christianity was introduced into Mercia and re-established among the East Saxons. The spread of Christianity was an important part of the activities of the Northumbrian bretwaldas although their position was none too safe until Penda's defeat. The Northumbrian contribution to English Christianity would have been adversely affected had Oswiu lost at Winwæd.

Oswiu's hand in the baptisms of Peada and Sigeberht was a continuation of a policy in which his predecessor Oswald stood as sponsor, or god father, to Cynegisl of the West Saxons who was baptised by Birinus about 635. Oswald in his capacity of overlord no doubt confirmed Cynegisl's grant of Dorchester on Thames to Birinus as an episcopal seat. The marriage sought by the heathen Peada to Oswiu's Christian daughter Alhflæd sequels the marriage between Edwin and Æthelburh since Oswiu would not agree to the marriage unless Peada converted. That he did so was in some measure due to the pressure of Alhfrith who was married to Peada's sister Cyneburh. (Cyneburh later founded and was first abbess of Caistor, Northamptonshire. After her death in about 680 she was succeeded by her sister Cyneswith). Peada together with his retinue were baptised by Finan at Ad Murum (Walton or Walbottle) near Hadrian's Wall in 653. On his return to Mercia Peada was accompanied by four priests. Three of them Cedd, Adda (brother of Utta abbot of Gateshead) and Betti were English and trained by Aidan, the fourth was the Irish Diuma. While Penda himself remained heathen he was not intolerant of Christianity provided that its adherents were committed. The Mercian church looked towards Lindisfarne rather than Canterbury. There is nothing to indicate that the Mercian church had any contact with Canterbury at this time and while the missionaries were Irish and English there is no suggestion of any conflict between them.

Sigeberht king of the East Saxons was a friend of Oswiu. During Sigeberht's visits to Northumbria Oswiu attempted to persuade him to become a Christian. The East Saxons had driven out Bishop Mellitus some forty years previously and remained heathen. Oswiu eventually succeeded and Sigeberht was baptised not long after Peada by Finan at the same place. Before returning home Sigeberht invited Oswiu to send missionaries to the East Saxons. Cedd was transferred from the Middle Angles to the East Saxons and remained responsible to Finan. The conversions of Peada and Sigeberht were thus consolidated by the work of Northumbrian missionaries, chiefly those from Lindisfarne, who had been trained by Aidan and subject to the authority of Lindisfarne.

After making headway Cedd returned to Lindisfarne for discussions with Finan. Learning of Cedd's success Finan had him consecrated bishop of the East Saxons. Cedd's bishopric was, like Aidan's, tribal with no fixed see. Bede says that Cedd " established churches in various places and ordained priests and deacons to assist him in preaching the word of faith and in the administration of baptism, especially in the city called Ythancæstir in the Saxon tongue [probably Othona, a Roman military settlement and now St Peter's on the Wall] and also in the place called Tilbury." At the former Cedd established a monastery on the Irish model. Precise dates for Cedd's activities are not known. Bede probably obtained much of his information about Cedd from the monks of Lastingham who presumably did not supply dates. During his East Saxon mission Cedd frequently visited Northumbria to preach and was introduced to Æthelwold sub-king of Deira by his (Cedd's) brother Cælin who was Æthelwold's chaplain. Cedd became a close friend of Æthelwold who granted him land on which he founded Lastingham which followed the observances of Lindisfarne. Its setting was austere if not as remote as Bede makes out and to be made suitable as a monastery it had to be cleansed of devils, an Irish practice. To accomplish this Cedd embarked on a fast of forty days corresponding to Christ's time in the wilderness. After thirty days Cedd was called to the king's court so his brother Cynebill completed the fast for him. Cedd returned to the East Saxons administering Lastingham through his representatives. Shortly after the Synod of Whitby when visiting Lastingham Cedd died during the great plague epidemic. He was buried on the right side of the altar there. On hearing of Cedd's death about thirty brothers transferred from his diocese among the East Saxons to Lastingham to be near his remains. Bede records that sadly, all of them died there of plague except one small, unnamed boy who as the result of Chad's prayers survived and went on to become a priest. Cedd had designated his brother Chad (Ceadda) as his successor at Lastingham. Bede notes that the four brothers were all famous priests and two became bishops, a rare occurrence in one family.

Irish and Roman ways began to combine in men like Cedd, Cuthbert and Wilfrid. A story is told by Bede of Cedd issuing a curse in an Irish manner. In it Bede, through his comments about Sigeberht's atonement, tries to soften the force of the situation. The reality of the king's death was not Cedd's curse but because in forgiving his enemies he failed to adhere to traditional English customs such as the wergild and highlights the difficulties inherent in the slow transition from pagan values to a Christian society:

> For a long time the instruction of the people in the heavenly life prospered day by day in the kingdom, to the joy of the king [Sigeberht] and the whole nation; but it then happened that the king was murdered, at the instigation of the enemy of all good men, by his own kinsmen. It was two brothers who perpetrated the crime. When they were asked why they did it, they could make no reply except that they were angry with the king and hated him because he was too ready to pardon his enemies, calmly forgiving them for the wrongs they had done him, as soon as they asked his pardon. Such was the crime for which he met his death, that he

had devoutly observed the gospel precepts. But nevertheless, by this innocent death a real offence was punished in accordance with the prophecy of the man of God. For one of these *gesiths* who murdered him was unlawfully married, a marriage which the bishop [Cedd] had been unable to prevent or correct. So he excommunicated him and ordered all who would listen to him not to enter the man's house nor take food with him. But the king disregarded this command and accepted an invitation of the *gesith* to dine at his house. As the king was coming away, the bishop met him. When the king saw him, he leapt from his horse and fell trembling at the bishop's feet, asking his pardon. The bishop, who was also on horseback, alighted too. In his anger he touched the prostrate king with his staff which he was holding in his hand, and exercising his episcopal authority, he uttered these words, 'I declare to you that, because you were unwilling to avoid the house of this man who is lost and damned, you will meet your death in this very house.' Yet we may be sure that the death of this religious king was such that it not only atoned for his offence but even increased his merit; for it came about as a result of his piety and his observance of Christ's command.

Columbanus in Gaul gave Theuderich the same sort of treatment and there are other similar stories. The occasion shows that Cedd, like Aidan, was a formidable character and, with his involvement in the king's court and Æthelwold's friendship, was not on the periphery of politics. Cedd's use of a horse shows the move away from strict adherence to Irish practices.

Bede mentions that Cedd served as interpreter at the Synod of Whitby. Possibly Bede felt that Cedd like Aidan recognised the importance of language in missionary work and that it reflected the humility of the church in the unity of tongues which made it possible for the apostles to understand Peter at the first Pentecost and all men to praise God in heaven.

Meanwhile in 656 after Peada's murder when Mercia was brought temporarily under Oswiu's rule Diuma was consecrated bishop of both the Mercians and Middle Angles by Finan. Bede says that because of the shortage of priests one bishop served both peoples. The see was first at Repton. Diuma's episcopacy was short. On his death he was succeeded by the Irish Ceollach who soon returned to Iona. Ceollach's successor was Trumhere of Gilling first bishop under Mercia's new king Wulfhere. His successor was Jaruman who in turn was succeeded by Chad.

Chad went to Ireland after his training at Lindisfarne under Aidan and spent some time with Egbert there before returning to Northumbria. After the Synod of Whitby Wilfrid went to the Continent and remained there for some time. In his continued absence Oswiu sent Chad then abbot of Lastingham to Canterbury to be consecrated bishop of York. With him went a priest called Eadhæd later bishop of Ripon. On arrival they found that Archbishop Deusdedit had died without a successor having been appointed. They went to the kingdom of the West Saxons and Chad was consecrated by Wine bishop of Winchester. Two British bishops participated in the consecration, evidence of co-operation between the two churches.

Oswiu and King Egbert of Kent chose the priest Wigheard one of Deusdedit's clergy as the new archbishop and sent him to Rome for consecration but Wigheard died of plague in Rome before he could be consecrated. Pope Vitalian wrote to Oswiu telling him about this and Bede reproduces the text which presumably was available to him in Northumbria rather than supplied from Canterbury. At the same time Vitalian sent Oswiu relics and Eanflæd a cross made from the fetters of Peter and Paul and a gold key. Theodore of Tarsus was consecrated as the new archbishop in 668.

Sometime after Wilfrid's return from Gaul Chad stood down from the York see conveniently and modestly regarding himself as unworthy of the job. Wulfhere asked Theodore for a bishop on Jaruman's death in 669. Chad was sent to Mercia after being reconsecrated. His original consecration was irregular because of the participation of British bishops. Their own consecrations were not regarded as canonical since in the British church unlike Roman practice only one bishop was needed to consecrate another. Only Wine was recognised by Wilfrid. Moreover Chad's original appointment had been to York a see (it was argued) which was not vacant. Wulfhere gave Chad fifty hides at At Baruae (At the Wood, possibly Barrow in Lincolnshire) where he built a monastery. Chad established his see at Lichfield instead of Repton but his episcopacy lasted only two and a half years for he died during yet another plague epidemic. Bede relates a story of Chad, typical of hagiography, involving the monk Owine. Owine had accompanied Æthelthryth a daughter of Anna, king of the East Angles, to Northumbria to marry Ecgfrith and joined Chad at Lastingham accompanying him to Lichfield. He was not a scholar but performed manual tasks. When Chad was in his oratory at his retreat Owine working outside heard heavenly music descending, entering the oratory and after about half an hour returning to heaven. Chad then sent Owine to summon the other brothers. On their arrival Chad exhorted them to live the Christian life telling them of his forthcoming death. After their departure Owine asked Chad about the heavenly music. Chad replied that they were angelic spirits who summoned him to heaven and were to return in seven days for this purpose. Chad immediately succumbed to the plague and died seven days later on 2 March 672. Bede adds that much later when Abbot Hygbald from Lindsey visited Egbert in Ireland and Chad's name was mentioned Egbert said he knew someone still living who at Chad's death saw the soul of Cedd descend with the angels to take his brother's soul to heaven. Chad was buried at Saint

Mary's Church in Lichfield but his remains were translated to the new church of Saint Peter which became Lichfield Cathedral. Miracles of healing were associated with both burial places:

> a madman, who had been wandering from one place to another, came there one evening unknown to or unregarded by the guardians of the church, and spent the whole night there. The next morning he came out in his right mind and, to the amazement and joy of all, demonstrated how he had regained his health there through the goodness of God. Chad's place of burial is a wooden coffin in the shape of a little house, having an aperture in its side, through which those who visit it out of devotion can insert their hands and take out a little of the dust. When it is put in water and given either to cattle or men who are ailing, they get their wish and are at once freed from their ailments and rejoice in health restored.

The passage contains one of the earliest descriptions of a saint's shrine.

Bede praises Chad for among other things his humility, prayer, poverty and right preaching and notes how he emulated Aidan singling out Chad's practice of travelling on foot. Bede also comments, recalling an earlier reference to Cedd on horseback, that Archbishop Theodore ordered Chad to ride on long journeys and personally assisted Chad in mounting a horse to underline the dignity of a bishop in the church of Rome and the obligation on Chad to run his diocese in accordance with Roman practices. Also following Irish ways at Lichfield Chad set up a retreat for himself where he could go with a small number of brothers. One of Bede's tutors Trumberht trained by Chad told Bede how Chad would pray to God for mercy and mankind if a gale arose and if the gale increased in violence or if there was a thunderstorm Chad's petitions were intensified. This reflects the Irish concern with nature noted in connection with Aidan. For Chad through the elements God reminded man of the awesome Last Judgment and provided an opportunity for self-examination.

CHAPTER 6

The Synod of Whitby

THERE ARE TWO ACCOUNTS OF THE SYNOD one by Eddius from information provided by Wilfrid and the other, longer and more structured, by Bede. As Bede presents it the Synod was primarily concerned with deciding between the Roman and Irish methods of calculating Easter. For him the Easter question was a matter of heresy and other differences between the churches are not given the same in-depth treatment. This does not however detract from Bede's attitude where there was a failure to conform or co-operate with the Roman church and its practices expressed in his account of the slaughter of the Bangor monks by Æthelfrith.

Information given by Bede about the differences between the churches other than Easter is distinctly limited. In his account of the conference at Augustine's Oak he says the British "did other things too which were not in keeping with the unity of the Church" and when recording Colman's succession to Finan alludes to "other matters of ecclesiastical discipline" before adding a reference to differences over the tonsure. After his account of the Synod Bede says that Colman (and others) who refused to accept Oswiu's decision left Northumbria coupling the tonsure to Easter as a source of dissent. The Irish shaved the front of the head leaving hair at the back whereas in the Roman church it was the crown which was shaved leaving the remaining circle of hair as a memorial of the crown of thorns. That the method of consecrating bishops was different between the two churches is evident from the need for Chad to be reconsecrated.

Another difference, that of baptism, is mentioned by Bede in the follow-up conference to that held at Augustine's Oak. Although precise details about baptism are not given by Bede it is possible that the concluding stages of the baptismal ceremony which involved anointing with sacred oil, laying on of hands and confirmation could be performed in non-Roman churches by priests as well as bishops but in the church of Rome only bishops could perform them. The only exception to the latter applied in rural areas where a bishop might not be available and occasional baptisms could be performed by some other cleric, a situation recognised by the Roman church. Further, in two occasions of baptism referred to by Bede both of which were at Easter which with Pentecost was regarded as the appropriate time, converts were baptized in rivers. But it was the font which was normally used for baptism and rivers are only mentioned by Bede in the context of mass baptisms. Baptism was probably usually by affusion, that is, water was poured over the head and streamed down the body, and thus did not involve total immersion. Portable fonts or cisterns for baptisms may well have been used in rural or remote areas to avoid the need to attend a distant church. These, together with the use of portable altars enabled visiting bishops to ensure conformity in baptismal ritual and to keep a close eye both on newly converted groups and conformity in doctrine.

The Easter debate itself involved a number of interlinked problems. Firstly, Christ's Resurrection was originally celebrated on the Jewish Passover, that is, on the fourteenth day of the first lunar month, Nisan, of the Jewish year ("lunar 14"). The church later considered that the Resurrection should not be celebrated on the same day as the Jewish Passover. Problems over deciding the date of Easter were tied up with differences between the lunar and solar calendars. To reconcile them extra lunar months which were of fixed length had to be added in to the calculations. Alexandrian computists used a 19 year cycle to achieve harmonization while slightly earlier an 8 year cycle had been devised along similar lines.

In the solar year "lunar 14" could occur in any day of the week in each succeeding year. The Council of Nicea in 325 ruled that Easter must be celebrated on a Sunday but not on the Passover. In avoiding the Passover the question was whether Easter should be celebrated on the Sunday after "lunar 14" which would then fall between "lunar 15" and "lunar 21". Under this system calculated by reference to lunar months, Easter would not fall before the vernal equinox and the earliest date of celebration would be 22 March. However, some time before Nicea the church of Rome had for some reason begun to celebrate Easter between "lunar 16" and "lunar 22". The dates on which Easter fell each year were calculated in advance and communicated by means of cycles of Easter tables of which there were three versions each derived from the same reconciliation of lunar and solar calendars. There was the 19 year cycle, an 84 year cycle used by the Irish church and the great cycle of 532 years developed in the mid fifth century by Victorius of Aquitaine in an attempt to eliminate any future discrepancies. Victorius also used *Annus Passionis* not *Anno Domini* dating. For his tables Victorius incorrectly used "lunar 16-22". Dionysius, responsible for *Anno Domini* dating, devised a system using 19 year cycles and applying "lunar 15-

21". After his system had been fully tested it was adopted by Rome in place of the system of Victorius sometime in the decade 630-40. In Northumbria the Irish 84 year cycle had been introduced by Aidan but as this cycle used "lunar 14" it meant that the Irish church celebrated Easter a week earlier than the Roman church. Simultaneously therefore with the observance of the Irish Easter James the Deacon was celebrating the Roman Easter. As Wilfrid did not learn of the Dionysian (or true) Easter until he arrived in Rome in 654 the Roman party in Northumbria would have been following the system devised by Victorius.

The significance of the different calculations lay in the reasoning that Christian unity was less meaningful if there was a lack of unanimity over the date of the principal festival. Yet the date for celebrating Easter was not the immediate cause of the Synod of Whitby. Relations between Augustine and the British bishops were not harmonious regardless of the Easter question and Aidan despite his contrary observance of Easter enjoyed universal respect. Evidence that Easter was really a cause of trouble in Northumbria before 661 is lacking. Bede does mention that the Irish Ronan who trained in Gaul and Italy zealously championed the Roman Easter but failed to persuade Finan to abandon the Irish Easter and that when Finan died in 661 the Easter debate resumed under his successor Colman. About 642 Oswiu who observed the Irish Easter married Eanflæd who was baptized by Paulinus and brought up in Kent, celebrated the Roman Easter. Whilst different dates for the celebration of Easter in the court of a bretwalda was strange there do not seem to have been any real problems over observances for either the king or queen. There had been plenty of opportunities to resolve differences. That nothing appears to have been done for more than twenty years suggests the matter was not overwhelmingly important and that Eanflæd was tolerant of her husband's adherence to the Irish Easter.

That the Synod was called was the probable upshot of an introduction effected by King Coenwalh of the West Saxons of Wilfrid to Oswiu's son Alhfrith, sub-king of Deira. Alhfrith was with his father an adherent of Irish Christianity but was influenced by and became the friend and partner of Wilfrid. Oswiu was not dissatisfied with his Irish Christianity and had no great enthusiasm for change. With Colman, Cedd and Hild on the Irish side Alhfrith was hard put to make a case for the benefit of the Roman faction and had to bring in the aged James the Deacon, the Frankish bishop Agilbert and his priest Agatho who were visiting Northumbria at the time and Eanflæd's chaplain Romanus. However Alhfrith's interest in the date of Easter was little more than superficial and political motives were involved. If Colman was forced out he could be replaced by someone, namely Wilfrid, belonging to the Roman faction under Alhfrith's patronage thereby weakening Oswiu's power and influence. Oswiu turned the tables on Alhfrith by deciding for the Roman Easter. Eddius comments that Oswiu gave his decision with a smile.

On the religious front the Synod did provide an opportunity for the churches to discuss their differences and the extent of their tolerance of each other's practices. Despite those differences the Irish church had its roots in the church of Rome. While there were differences over practices the fundamentals of belief were not in dispute.

Whitby was a suitable venue in view of its connections with the Northumbrian royal families; its abbess was Hild and Ælflæd was under her charge. In the presence of abbots, priests and other ecclesiastics Oswiu opened the debate and invited Colman to speak first. Colman appealed to tradition for the Irish calculation of Easter arguing that Irish customs originated with the apostle John. Oswiu then asked Agilbert to justify the origin and authority of Roman customs. Agilbert although the senior ecclesiastic present felt that linguistic differences would create problems of communication and sought Oswiu's permission for Wilfrid to represent the united Roman view in English. Wilfrid pointed to the authority of universal practice observing that the only dissenters were the Irish present, the Picts and British. He held that the apostle John correctly observed Easter but that Colman and his party did not in fact follow John and went on to dismiss Colman's appeal to Anatolius to whom a tract, from which the 84 year cycle had been adopted, had been incorrectly attributed. As to Colman's predecessors including Columba Wilfrid recognised that they knew no different, although had they known they would have changed, whereas Colman did have the benefit of knowledge and should not ignore the fact. Despite his holiness Columba could not be cited against Peter the rock of Christ's church and holder of the keys of heaven. Colman, when asked by Oswiu, could not deny Peter's precedence and was thereby isolated particularly since the church in southern Ireland had earlier adopted the Roman Easter. Although the Synod has been viewed as a local affair Oswiu's decision in favour of Rome facilitated the unification of the English church under Archbishop Theodore and enabled Northumbria to participate in the church's missionary work in the years ahead. Direct links between Northumbria and Rome increased too. At the same time the outcome of the Synod did not affect relations or contacts with Ireland and it did not eradicate Irish influences and traditions in Northumbria.

Colman refused to adopt the Roman Easter and returned to Iona with his fellow Irish monks and about thirty English monks whom he had trained. He moved from Iona to the small island of Inishboffin where he founded a monastery in about 667 housing both Irish and English monks. Following dissension caused by Irish monks wandering off in summer and returning later to enjoy what the English had harvested colman founded a monastery at Mayo for the English monks leaving the Irish at Inishboffin. Colman died about 675. In Bede's time English monks were still at Mayo which had become a distinguished community and had a rule and canonically elected abbot.

Tuda who accepted the outcome of the Synod succeeded Colman as bishop of Lindisfarne. He had been trained and consecrated in southern Ireland and had come to Northumbria during Colman's episcopate. Eata, abbot of Melrose and one of the English boys trained by Aidan, was appointed abbot of Lindisfarne by Oswiu at the behest of the departing Colman. Soon after his appointment Tuda died during the plague of 664 and was buried in the unidentified monastery of Pægnalæch.

In his treatment of the Easter issue the unity of the Roman church was fundamental for Bede. The Easter debate was also related to his love of Irish scholarship and close interest in computistical issues. In the latter the contents of a letter written between 632 and 636 by Cummian abbot of Durrow attempting to persuade Segene abbot of Iona to adopt the Roman Easter found an echo in Wilfrid's arguments at Whitby. In the *Ecclesiastical History* the Synod is followed, not accidentally, by an account of the work of the Englishman Egbert. During the episcopates of Finan and Colman many English nobles and ordinary people travelled to Ireland to study or live the monastic life. Among the nobles were Æthelhun, brother of that Æthelwine, who also subsequently went to Ireland and became bishop of Lindsey, and Egbert. These two lost many of their companions through plague and themselves succumbed to it. Egbert prayed that he would survive until he could atone for past sins and vowed he would never return home. While Æthelhun died, Egbert survived to become a priest working among the Picts and Irish. In 716 Egbert arrived at Iona and persuaded the monks there to adopt the Roman Easter and tonsure after Adomnan had previously failed. Bede refers to Egbert as a bishop. It is unlikely that his primacy extended over the Irish of Iona since the occupant of the bishop's seat there at the time is known. Egbert died on Iona, appropriately at Easter, in 729 at the age of ninety.

CHAPTER 7

Cuthbert

CUTHBERT WAS POPULAR NOT ONLY IN NORTHUMBRIA but elsewhere in England and on the Continent. Much of what is known about him is to be found in prose *Lives* compiled by a monk of Lindisfarne whose identity is not known and Bede. There are seven surviving manuscripts of the former, the earliest dating to the late ninth or early tenth century, and thirty six of the Bede of which the earliest comes from the beginning of the tenth century.

The Lindisfarne monk based his *Life of Saint Cuthbert* on what information was available about Cuthbert at Lindisfarne and references within its text show that it was written between the elevation of Cuthbert's remains in 698 and Aldfrith's death in 705. Bede based his own *Life* of about 721 on the Lindisfarne version. He says that he had made the most rigorous investigation of the facts and his notes, or first draft, were shown to Herefrith abbot of Lindisfarne on visiting Jarrow and to others who had known Cuthbert. After making amendments in the light of observations made Bede wrote up his *Life* and passed it for further consideration to Lindisfarne where it was read for two days before the teachers and elders there. This vetting process not only gave the Lindisfarne community the opportunity to check the detail it also reflected the community's concern that Cuthbert's character was presented in the best light without flaws or weaknesses.

Bede refers in his prose work to an earlier metrical *Life of Saint Cuthbert* he had written and which still survives. In producing these two versions Bede was following a precedent set by Sedulius while in the later one he was fulfilling his intention of providing a fuller account of his subject. His prose *Life* closely follows the anonymous Lindisfarne one to begin with but rearranges the order of the miracles and provides an extended account of Cuthbert's death together with a quantity of additional material. In his prologue Bede does not acknowledge his use of the anonymous *Life* and does not quote its sources anywhere. He does however identify the sources of his additional material taking care to differentiate between eyewitness and second-hand accounts. Bede's *Life* is the more sophisticated of the two works but it is not necessarily better.

For his work Bede asks the Lindisfarne community that prayers are said and masses celebrated for him after his death. This has already been promised and Guthfrith the sacrist (later abbot) asked to place his name in the *Liber Vitæ* or *Book of life*. The *Liber Vitæ* was a list of names of people both living and dead for whom the Lindisfarne community said prayers during mass. Although the original version has not survived a copy made in the ninth century is preserved in the British Museum. Both *Lives* were dedicated to Eadfrith, bishop of Lindisfarne (698-721).

Cuthbert was of English stock born about 634, the year in which Oswald defeated Cadwallon. From the age of eight Cuthbert was placed with a foster mother Coenswith in the village of Hruringaham which was probably near Melrose. He is portrayed as a particularly energetic youth playing games with his peers. From fairly early on he seems to have suffered from synovitis of the knee. At the time of Aidan's death Cuthbert was looking after sheep on hills near the river Leader which flows into the Tweed. This occupation should not be taken to imply that Cuthbert was of peasant stock. In Bede's *Life* there is a reference to him riding a horse and holding a spear which he handed to his servant, a clue that he belonged to the nobility. This is reinforced by his being fostered since it was mainly children of the nobility who were so placed. Before giving up secular life Cuthbert was in military service. The anonymous *Life* tells of him in an army encampment at a time of enemy threat. On various occasions Penda raided Northumbria and this may have been one of them. It is unlikely to have been at the time of Penda's defeat at Winwæd since Cuthbert entered Melrose in, or very soon after, 651.

Cuthbert was received at Melrose monastery by the prior Boisil and a certain Sigfrith. This was not the Sigfrith who was also at Melrose and later became abbot of Wearmouth. Eata was abbot. Little is known of Cuthbert's time at Melrose. Most of the material in the *Lives* concentrates on the Lindisfarne years and reflects the interest of its monks in their own monastery not Melrose. According to the Lindisfarne writer Cuthbert took his vows at Ripon but Bede puts this at Melrose and this is more likely. The reference to Ripon was probably due to confusion. King Alhfrith gave land for a monastery at Ripon to which Eata and a group of monks including Cuthbert transferred. Cuthbert was appointed guestmaster, an acknowledgement of his tact and ability to get on with people, essential qualities for an office which involved contact with those from the outside world. Refusing to adopt Roman practices they vacated Ripon returning to Melrose about 660. Boisil then died of plague to which Cuthbert succumbed (but survived). Cuthbert succeeded Boisil as prior and following his example preached in neighbouring towns and also remote villages where others would not go, correcting those who had abandoned Christianity or practised pagan customs. Cuthbert is described as a skilful teacher and, travelling usually on foot but sometimes on horseback, would often be away for a week, sometimes for two or three weeks or even a month. On one occasion Cuthbert journeyed to the unidentified territory of the Niduari people among the Picts in the company of two brothers one of whom was a priest Tydi the source of four stories about Cuthbert. (Unlike other saints in the Irish tradition Cuthbert does not seem to have held strong views about travelling on horseback).

Plecgisl a priest at Melrose tells how Æbbe invited Cuthbert to visit her at Coldingham. During the visit a cleric followed Cuthbert to the seashore at night and watched him go into a stormy sea up to his armpits. This was a customary feature of asceticism practised by Wilfrid and Dryhthelm. Dryhthelm, a family man, had entered Melrose following a vision experienced during an illness in which he died and after witnessing the torments of the damned and the abodes of the blessed spirits returned to life. This type of vision was not unusual. That of Fursa is described by Bede in the *Ecclesiastical History* and Boniface in one of his letters provides another example. Dryhthelm used to talk to King Aldfrith, Æthelwold, then abbot, and a monk of Melrose Hæmgisl about his vision. Bede relates how Dryhthelm would stand in the Tweed for severe bodily penance and plunge repeatedly under the water while reciting psalms and prayers. In the winter with the ice swirling around him he used to reply to those who marvelled at him, "I have known it colder".

After the Synod of Whitby Eata became abbot and Cuthbert prior of Lindisfarne holding their offices at Melrose simultaneously. In 676 Cuthbert left Lindisfarne with the consent of his abbot for Inner Farne. He had already spent some time in seclusion traditionally on Saint Cuthbert's Isle but he needed somewhere more remote. Aidan had used Farne for short periods of retreat and others had tried unsuccessfully to inhabit Farne on their own. Cuthbert cleansed Farne of the devils which inhabited it, as Cedd had done at Lastingham, before building a dwelling area. This was circular with a high outer wall of unworked stones and turf and a dug out floor. Within it there was an oratory, some small huts and a spring. The layout, which was followed by John of Beverley for his retreat near Hexham, displays a number of influences. The wall was a feature of Coptic monasteries and the huts were similar to those used by Egyptian hermits while the use of large stones may have been Irish and the dug out floor pre-Christian. At the landing place was a reception area with a well. There is mention of a twelve foot beam which was washed ashore and used for building a closet for visitors. Cuthbert could utilize materials whatever their source. Until he could produce his own food he lived on what was brought by visitors. He was more successful with barley than wheat but was pestered by birds eating the seed he had sown.

Cuthbert was regarded with such reverence that visitors came not only from Lindisfarne but other, more distant parts of the country. Bede tells how Cuthbert would wash his visitors' feet in warm water and how he would keep his boots on from one Easter to the next only taking them off for the ritual washing of feet on Maundy Thursday. In consequence of this and his genuflexions a long, thick callus developed between his feet and shins although it has been suggested this was a symptom of the probable condition of which he died. From Farne Cuthbert went to meet Ælfflæd on Coquet Island a convenient venue between Whitby and Farne well known for its companies of monks. It was not their only meeting and serves, with his visits to Æbbe, Iurminburh and his foster mother, to show that he was on good terms with women. His talks with Ælfflæd emphasize that he was not untouched by politics. Cuthbert warned Ecgfrith against his campaign of 685, perhaps in a manner reminiscent of Cedd's treatment of Sigeberht and suggesting that Cuthbert was no less a formidable figure. The king's policies were no doubt on the agenda on Coquet Island as was the succession. Cuthbert at the least implied his allegiance to Ælfflæd who sided with Aldfrith and was a leading member of the faction which secured his accession. He mixed in court circles and was a confidant of Iurminburh whereas Wilfrid was not.

A synod presided over by Ecgfrith which met in 684 near the river Aln at Adtuifyrdi, the place of the double ford (possibly Alnmouth or Whittingham) elected Cuthbert bishop in place of Tunberht of Hexham. Trumwine, bishop of Abercorn, visited Cuthbert to tell him about his appointment and to persuade him to accept it. It was Trumwine, together with Elias, a Lindisfarne priest, who provided the author of the anonymous *Life* with the information about Cuthbert's youth. Cuthbert's reluctance in accepting the office of bishop was characteristic of other saints. He was consecrated in Ecgfrith's presence by Archbishop Theodore at York assisted by six other bishops on Easter Day 685. Eata's seat was at Lindisfarne which Cuthbert preferred so by mutual agreement they exchanged seats. Although Cuthbert was one of those who preferred to give up Ripon monastery rather than change their Irish practices he did accept the outcome of the Synod of Whitby. He acknowledged the authority of the archbishop of Canterbury and recognized the need for order and unity within the church. Roman and Irish ways came together in Cuthbert and his flexibility over Whitby made him politically acceptable.

Within two months of his consecration Cuthbert, accompanied by a group of priests and deacons, began a visitation of his diocese. On his way to Carlisle at the same time as Ecgfrith was attacking the Picts and where he visited

Iurminburh he pitched tents in a district called Ahse and visited a village Bedesfeld where he resettled nuns after they had abandoned their monastery in the face of Pictish forces. At Bedesfeld he was attended by Æthelwold who served Cuthbert as a novice (as Wilfrid served Cudda) and who became prior and abbot of Melrose before becoming bishop of Lindisfarne. He was also reported at Medilwong during a plague epidemic in the village and in another district called Kintis accompanied by a priest Beta.

After two years as bishop Cuthbert, in failing health and no longer able to carry out his episcopal duties, returned to Farne. Bede gives a much more detailed account of Cuthbert's last days than the Lindisfarne monk having received an eye witness account from Herefrith. Herefrith had been at Melrose when Cuthbert took his vows and when Boisil died. Listed in the *Liber Vitæ* Herefrith relinquished his office as abbot of Lindisfarne to become a hermit. Two months after Cuthbert's retirement when Herefrith was visiting him his health deteriorated. He provided Herefrith with burial instructions. His body was to be wrapped in the winding sheet given by Verca abbess of South Shields and buried in the sarcophagus provided by Cudda stored nearby. Cuthbert was not willing for anyone to stay with him although no-one was able to return to Farne straightaway because of bad weather. When after five days a group of monks landed on Farne they found Cuthbert sitting in the visitor's reception area at the landing stage where he could be easily found. During those five days he kept five onions to quench his thirst but had consumed only one half of one of them. Herefrith bathed the swelling on Cuthbert's foot with warm water, treated the suppurating ulcer which had developed on the swelling and gave him some warm wine. Leaving some brothers, among whom was a priest Beda the elder who is specifically mentioned, with Cuthbert Herefrith briefly returned to Lindisfarne when he informed the community of Cuthbert's wish to be buried on Farne. Back on Farne Herefrith sought to persuade Cuthbert to be buried on Lindisfarne but Cuthbert felt this would be troublesome for the Lindisfarne community on account of his reputation. Finally Cuthbert agreed but on condition that he was buried in the church there so that the monks could decide which visitors should have access to his tomb. The visitors referred to would not only be pilgrims but could include fugitives and the guilty seeking sanctuary. A church had a special right of sanctuary where it possessed a saint's relics and this came to be held at Hexham (Acca), Tynemouth (Oswine), Ripon (Wilfrid) and Beverley (John) and much later Durham where Cuthbert's remains finally came to rest.

Like Bede, Cuthbert on his deathbed gave instructions for the distribution of such effects as he possessed. Unable to walk Cuthbert was carried back to his dwelling. After receiving the sacraments he died, probably of tuberculosis, on the evening of Wednesday 20 March 687. News of his death was communicated to Lindisfarne by the lighting of torches, a prearranged signal. His body was taken to Lindisfarne and washed in preparation for burial. His head was wrapped in a head cloth, the unconsecrated host placed on his breast and his body was robed in priestly garments and shoes put on his feet. After being swathed in the winding sheet he was buried in the sarcophagus in Lindisfarne church.

The anonymous *Life* emphasizes Cuthbert's humility and poverty and holds up the ideal of the monk while at the time maintaining the dignity of a bishop. In listing Cuthbert's virtues the writer follows Isidore of Seville's view of the qualities needed by a bishop. They were in turn used of Wilfrid by Eddius. This sort of borrowing emphasizes that, strictly biographical data apart, a substantial part of the material on Cuthbert is not to be taken literally as fact but needs to be regarded with caution. The particular models for the lives of Cuthbert and earlier saints were Athanasius' *Life of Saint Anthony* and Severus' *Life of Saint Martin* copies of which were available at Lindisfarne and Jarrow. A quantity of material was derived, for example, from Jerome's *Life of Saint Paul* and the lives of Saint Benedict and Augustine as well as the Bible. The very beginning of the anonymous *Life* is taken from Severus and Athanasius. As well as having precedents elsewhere some of the incidents in Cuthbert's life have been worked in such a way as to make a specific point. A notable instance of this is Cuthbert's final speech in which Bede has him warning against Irish heresies especially not celebrating Easter at the proper time. The saint's last words amounted to a literary convention which could be employed as a medium for conveying a writer's own views. Thus, with Bede's preoccupation with the Easter issue the speech he ascribes to Cuthbert comes as no surprise.

Prophecies and visions were a common feature of hagiography and they can be found also in Cuthbert's *Lives*. In his youth while playing games, his future as a bishop was anticipated by a three year old child who told him he should behave with more fitting dignity. As Eddius and Alcuin were later to do, the Lindisfarne monk draws parallels with the biblical characters of Samuel, David, Jeremiah and John the Baptist. When among the Niduari Cuthbert himself foretold tempest and calm. The ability to prophesy was a mark of growing spiritual power. He foretold Ecgfrith's death as Aidan had Oswine's and Cedd Sigeberht's. However, Cuthbert had warned Ecgfrith of the folly of his campaign so the outcome was not surprising and with hindsight the claim to prophecy here is rather thin. Moreover with an understanding of political realities, the failure by a king to deal effectively with his opponents in his kingdom is a case in point, it would not be too difficult to predict events. Prior knowledge of their own deaths was quite usual among saints and Cuthbert with Chad and Wilfrid was no exception. At Carlisle Cuthbert told the anchorite Hereberht that they could not expect to meet again in this life. Hereberht pleaded that he might die at the same time as Cuthbert. After suffering a long illness his wish was granted. With deteriorating health or an outbreak of plague survival could not be expected but it is possible that saints foretelling their own deaths were expressing apprehension of sudden demise without having received communion.

The visions too are of a type with Cuthbert having simultaneous knowledge of events elsewhere. While on a tour of Carlisle's Roman remains conducted by Waga the reeve Cuthbert on observing the state of the sky knew that God had judged against the English. During another meeting with Ælfflæd at a place called Ovington apparently not far from Whitby he went into a trance and saw the death of a monk Hadwald who had fallen from a tree. There is the familiar story of how Cuthbert when looking after sheep had a vision of angels carrying a holy soul to heaven. Bede says he learned of Aidan's death the following morning while the Lindisfarne monk puts this several days later. The latter is more likely since Aidan died at Bamburgh and it would have taken a little while for news of his death to reach those living near the river Leader. Angels had an important role for Cuthbert's biographers for they appear in the lives of Irish saints, appeared to Saint Martin and, older still, were of assistance to anchorites in the Egyptian desert. Frequently in accounts of saints including Northumbrian saints their souls are taken to heaven by angels.

Miracles and fondness for wildlife have always been dominant associations with Cuthbert in the popular mind. This love of nature and friendship with animals and birds are to be found in Egyptian and Irish traditions. When Cuthbert was observed in the sea at Coldingham sea animals ministered to him. Bede refers to the animals as otters which in Ireland were regarded as possessing magical properties. The following day when the cleric confessed what he had seen Cuthbert told him not to mention it to anyone. This prohibition, also in accounts of Chad and Willibrord, is rooted in the New Testament and Christ's transfiguration and could be used as a saint's cult was developing to overcome the problem of why nothing was known about such episodes at the time they occurred. On a later occasion Cuthbert saw two ravens removing material from the roof of his reception area to make their nest. He banished them but one returned in penitence after three days so he allowed them to stay. In return they brought him some swine's lard which his visitors used to grease their boots for a year. A similar story is told by Severus.

Miracles occur at every turn of Cuthbert's life even in the most ordinary situations. Angels, again, are featured in two advocating a hot poltice to cure a tumour of the knee and helping to move the large stones used to construct the outer wall of his dwelling on Farne. The twelve foot beam was miraculously washed ashore there at the precise spot where it was needed and a spring appeared in the rock after his visitors' prayers, a story told of Moses and Saints Anthony and Benedict.

Much the same can be said of the miracles of Cuthbert as those of Aidan and Oswald. Broadly they fall into four groups or types. One is the provision of food. When travelling northwards during a storm in winter to Chester-le-Street Cuthbert stopped to shelter at an unoccupied hut. His horse disturbed the roof and a warm loaf and some meat fell from it. This Lindisfarne version is elaborated by Bede who has Cuthbert going first to a house of a religious woman. She offers Cuthbert some food but he refuses. Unable to complete his journey that day he then stops at an unoccupied shepherd's hut where he receives the food. Bede, told the story by Ingwold a Wearmouth priest who had it from Cuthbert personally, has changed the emphasis of the story from God providing Cuthbert with food in a remote place to God's recognition of Cuthbert's rectitude in refusing to break his fast while travelling. Significantly the day was a Friday which with Wednesday was a fast day. During his visit to the Picts three portions of dolphin flesh were found by the water's edge. When preaching in a remote area an eagle settled on the banks of the river Teviot. Cuthbert's companion, a boy, discovered it had a large fish which he wrested from it. Cuthbert asked the boy why he did not let the fisherman have his share so the boy returned half the fish to the eagle. There are other similar instances and it is not difficult to recognize their biblical origin, the feeding of the five thousand and Elijah receiving food from ravens especially. The finding of the dolphin flesh occurred at Epiphany when the feeding of the five thousand and the turning of water into wine (another Cuthbert parallel) were celebrated.

Two stories have burning houses as their subject. In one the walls of a house were demolished to extinguish the flames but the fire was an illusion. Illusory fires can be found in Irish stories and elsewhere and have their origin in the burning bush although they can also be the work of the devil as with this one. This type of incident and the purifying of monastic and similar sites stress the fight with devils. This was an essential part of the warfare engaged in by the Christian soldier, often the monk, a prominent theme in Bede's writing. In the second story Cuthbert was visiting his foster mother when a house at the east end of the village caught fire. The remaining dwellings were threatened because of a strong easterly wind. Coenswith begged his help. Cuthbert imitating saints Martin, Benedict and Aidan prayed, the wind direction changed and the threat was averted. A sequel in which, again, good fortune perhaps rather than the miraculous is translated into Cuthbert's ability to control the forces of nature. Events related to Bede by Bælla a fellow monk at Jarrow are set at a monastery near the mouth of the Tyne on the south side once occupied by men but subsequently taken over by nuns. It was probably South Shields whose abbess was Verca and where Cuthbert drank from a cup in which water turned to wine. A group of monks were transporting wood for their monastery by raft. About to land a sudden gale swept them and their rafts off towards the river mouth. Some other monks were hindered from assisting due to the force of the current and wind. A crowd on the north bank stood jeering. They were contemptuous of the monks whom they regarded as responsible for repressing their old, pagan, religion, evidence for the slow adoption of Christianity in some parts. Cuthbert standing among the crowd prayed. The wind changed and the monks returned safely to the river bank.

Finally, Cuthbert performed acts of healing as part of his ministry. Alongside the other material the healing miracles help to build up a picture of Cuthbert's movements supplying names of people and places. One or two examples of these miracles will suffice. At Bedesfeld, Cuthbert cured a kinswoman of Bishop Æthelwold of some form of paralysis. It is only occasionally that symptoms are described in any detail and rarely that there is any indication of the long-term success of the miracle. Hildmer a reeve of Ecgfrith (which thus dates the story to sometime after 670), asked Cuthbert to cure his wife who was vexed by a devil. Hildmer did not disclose the nature of the illness but Cuthbert knew and declared, correctly, that she would be well by the time they arrived at Hildmer's house. Subsequently Hildmer was cured of an unspecified illness by drinking water in which bread had been dropped after Cuthbert blessed it. Similarly, during Aldfrith's reign the wife of Hemma a gesith was cured when water blessed by Cuthbert was sprinkled over her by his priest.

Cuthbert's last act of healing was to cure a sufferer of dysentery Walhstod one of the group from Lindisfarne with him when he died. Various miracles were attributed to Cuthbert after his death. They are in much the same vein as some of those reported during his lifetime and those posthumously credited to Oswald for they are of a conventional type in hagiography. A poisoned boy whom Tydi was unable to cure drank water which contained earth from the place where Cuthbert's body had been washed while a paralytic boy was cured when shoes Cuthbert had worn were put on his feet. Baduthegn who served in the guesthouse at Lindisfarne was cured of a seizure through prayer and a brother from a new monastery at Dacre near Penrith was cured of a tumour on the eyelid by touching it with some of Cuthbert's hair. A member of Willibrord's *familia* fell ill during a visit to Lindisfarne but recovered on being taken to Cuthbert's relics. On the eleventh anniversary of his death, 20 March 698, with the sanction of Bishop Eadberht then in retreat on Saint Cuthbert's Isle Cuthbert's remains were elevated. When the sarcophagus was opened his body was found to be incorrupt. Bede records another exhumation, that of Æthelthryth at Ely when the remains were discovered in a similar state. Some embalming process is the most natural explanation but for

Bede an incorrupt body is linked with purity in life. That Cuthbert's body had not decomposed must have had a great impact in an age when there was a deep rooted belief in the miraculous and this was an essential and key factor in the development of his cult.

CHAPTER 8

Wilfrid

THE *LIFE OF BISHOP WILFRID* WAS WRITTEN not long after Wilfrid's death and probably by 720. The author gives his name as Stephen the priest. Bede refers to an Æddi surnamed Stephen who was invited from Kent by Wilfrid and, apart from James the Deacon, he was the first singing master in the Northumbrian churches. Although the attribution is not decisive it is this Eddius who is thought to have been Wilfrid's biographer.

Eddius probably came to Northumbria in 669 and accompanied Wilfrid on his last journey to Rome subsequently returning to Ripon where, according to references in the *Life*, he was a monk. The *Life* was commissioned by "my venerable masters Bishop Acca and Abbot Tatberht" who were probably Eddius' sources as were the monks who knew and supported Wilfrid (Eddius says his work was written on "good authority" and "tested by trustworthy men"). The anonymous *Life of Cuthbert* was a likely motivation for the production at Ripon of a rival work about Wilfrid. Eddius' preface is taken almost completely from the *Life of Cuthbert* which in turn borrows from other writers. However Eddius' *Life* is much superior in quality to the anonymous *Life of Cuthbert*, more comparable with Bede's *Lives of the Abbots*. Bede made use of Eddius' *Life* and obtained information personally from Wilfrid about Æthelthryth and from Acca about the visit to Willibrord. Eddius' account is apologetic in nature. He was biased, distorting the facts to present Wilfrid, whom he greatly admired, in the best light. Bede takes a less personal, more detached view, to some extent contrasting the world of politics and dynastic rivalries against which Eddius sets Wilfrid with his own quieter monastic world and although the miraculous represents only a small fraction of Eddius' *Life* Bede noticeably plays down the miraculous in his material on Wilfrid but plays it up in his *Life of Cuthbert*. Nevertheless Bede is first and foremost a historian and, apart from supplying additional material, can usually be considered more reliable where there are differences between himself and

Eddius. The earliest manuscript of Eddius' *Life* in the British Museum is mainly ninth century originating from Yorkshire.

Wilfrid (or Wilfrith) was born in, or close to, 634. Eddius presents him as predestined by God for his work comparing him with Jeremiah and has a heavenly fire over the house at Wilfrid's birth, a parallel with Moses and the burning bush. There was a precedent for the latter in the lives of the saints, including those of Columba and Cuthbert belonging to the Irish tradition. At the age of fourteen with his father's agreement Wilfrid decided to pursue the religious life. His own mother had died and it seems he had a stepmother with whom he did not get on. Wilfrid went under the direction of Eanflæd to Lindisfarne in about 648 as a companion or servant of one of the king's thegns named Cudda who suffered some form of paralysis and who was leaving the court to become a monk there. It was probably this Cudda who provided Cuthbert with the sarcophagus in which he was buried and who is referred to in the anonymous *Life of Cuthbert* as Abbot Cudda.

At Lindisfarne Wilfrid "learned the whole Psalter by heart as well as several books" but he did not receive the tonsure at this stage. About 652 Wilfrid left Lindisfarne for Rome. With a letter of commendation from Queen Eanflæd Wilfrid arrived at the court of King Eorcenberht of Kent, her cousin (Honorius was then archbishop), and remained there until a suitable companion could be found. A year later Benedict Baducing arrived in Kent on his way to Rome and was prepared to take Wilfrid with him. They travelled to Lyons and were hospitably received by the archbishop whose name Eddius says was Dalfinus. It is likely that Eddius is confused here since Dalfinus was count of Lyons and it was his brother Aunemundus who was archbishop. Bede says Wilfrid delayed here while Benedict went on. Aunemundus offered Wilfrid his niece in marriage (and, Bede adds, the administration of a large area) but Wilfrid declined because he had chosen another way of life and resumed his journey.

In 654 Wilfrid reached Rome. His and Benedict's was the first known visit there by the English. In Rome he received the pope's blessing, studied under Archdeacon Boniface and learnt of the Roman method of calculating Easter. He then returned to Lyons where he stayed for three years receiving the tonsure from the archbishop. As the result of civil strife the archbishop was murdered in a revolution instigated by Ebroin, mayor of the palace in Neustria, and Wilfrid's life was at risk but he was spared because he was of the English race. Wilfrid could not remain at Lyons and so returned home. On his arrival Alhfrith sub-king in Deira, granted Wilfrid ten hides "in a place called Stamford" and not long after that the monastery at Ripon with thirty hides. According to Eddius Alhfrith introduced Wilfrid, described as abbot of Ripon, to Agilbert and at Alhfrith's request Agilbert consecrated Wilfrid priest. Agilbert had succeeded Birinus as bishop of the West Saxons but King Coenwalh not understanding his speech brought in Wine and so split Agilbert's diocese. As a result Agilbert left and was visiting Northumbria at the time of the Synod of Whitby. Alhfrith wanted Wilfrid as bishop in succession to Colman but Tuda succeeded Colman. Eddius ignores Tuda's brief episcopate. Oswiu may have been taken off guard by Tuda's premature death which opened the way for Wilfrid. Wilfrid went to Gaul for consecration, most likely to ensure that it would be canonically valid. The consecration which took place at Compiègne was an event of great state. Twelve bishops, including Agilbert (by then bishop of Paris), were involved in the consecration and "raising him aloft in accordance with their custom as he sat in the golden chair, the bishops unaided alone carried him with their own hands into the oratory, chanting hymns and songs in chorus". There is symbolism here of Christ and the twelve apostles.

Wilfrid delayed in Gaul for some time. On crossing from Gaul Eddius says that a storm arose (as with the disciples at Galilee) and Wilfrid's ship was driven to the shore of the pagan South Saxons. In a vivid passage with the pagans' chief priest cursing Wilfrid and his companions, Wilfrid's party fought victoriously against the heathen. Their ship was refloated and they reached Sandwich in safety.

Eddius' account of the fight with its parallel with David and Goliath is clothed in references to the Old Testament. The extensive Old Testament allusions by Eddius in his *Life* are not accidental (and those in Alcuin's *Life of Willibrord* might be considered in a similar light) and show a concern with salvation at a time of intensive evangelism. The allusions serve to illustrate the influences on Wilfrid at Lindisfarne, Gaul and Rome. It can be shown that Bede in his commentaries on books of the Old Testament provides interpretations of many of the allusions by Eddius. Moreover Bede's commentaries were written for Acca who was one of those who commissioned Eddius' *Life*. This *Life* and Bede's commentaries were written more or less at a time when Acca did much to stimulate scholarship so that in Eddius hagiography and exegesis are brought together. The frequent use of Old Testament allusions can be taken further. For Eddius the Old Testament could provide an understanding of Wilfrid comparable with the different ways it could yield of seeing Christ. In his approach Eddius was following Severus' *Life of Saint Martin*. If as is probable Eddius presents Wilfrid as Wilfrid would have presented himself it could be that Wilfrid's career was fashioned on the Old Testament and also that Wilfrid followed the desert ascetics who themselves emulated the Old Testament prophets both in their public lives and in their seclusion. At Lindisfarne Wilfrid would have encountered Irish asceticism and its related concept of pilgrimage which manifested itself in missionary work. He would also have encountered asceticism in Gaul. Wilfrid's own asceticism can be seen in several examples.

Eddius says that in feasting he was abstemious and at Eorcenberht's court in Kent he prayed and fasted. Eddius observes that Wilfrid washed in holy water at night during both summer and winter into his later years when Pope John put an end to this practice and has anchorites present when Wilfrid died to reinforce his approval of ascetics.

Wilfrid in his response reported by Eddius declining Archbishop Aunemundus' invitation to stay at Lyons refers to Abraham in the context of his wish to continue his journey to Rome. Abraham was an appropriate allusion for Irish pilgrims travelling to Rome in the period. Further Wilfrid through what he was to learn in Rome links pilgrimage to service to the nation, a connection made again later in the *Life*.

When Wilfrid found his seat occupied by Chad he retired to Ripon. During his time there he was occasionally invited to Mercia by King Wulfhere to carry out episcopal duties. Wilfrid similarly at Egbert's request visited Kent where prior to Theodore's arrival in England he ordained priests and deacons. He brought to Northumbria Eddius and Æona to teach the Roman chant together with "masons and artisans of almost every kind". It was at this point that Wilfrid introduced in Northumbria the rule of Saint Benedict which tempered the ascetic excesses of the Irish church.

After becoming archbishop Theodore began re-ordering the English church in a series of visitations. It was during Theodore's visit to Northumbria that to allow Wilfrid's restoration Chad stood down from York and returned to Lastingham. According to Bede Theodore was responsible for Chad's transfer to Mercia not Wilfrid as Eddius has it. While biased towards Wilfrid Eddius nevertheless reflects the high esteem in which Chad was held. Wilfrid was bishop of the whole of Northumbria from 669 to 677.

In this period, the precise date is unknown but it may have been about 672, Wilfrid built his church at Ripon which Eddius regarded as "a marvel of beauty hitherto unheard of in our times". Eddius refers to its dressed stone, columns and side aisles and altar vested in purple and gold. He tells how Wilfrid had ordered, for the welfare of his soul, the four gospels to be written in letters of pure gold on purple parchment and illuminated and that he had "ordered jewellers to construct for the books a case all made of purest gold and set with most precious gems". He describes the dedication which was attended by the king and dignitaries of every kind including sub-kings, reeves and abbots. Wilfrid read out the royal charters by which he had been made grants as well as a list of various consecrated places under his control which the British clergy had deserted when fleeing from English warriors. "There was great feasting lasting for three days and nights".

Wilfrid also restored the church in York founded by Edwin and completed by Oswald. It had fallen into decay perhaps because it was not given much

63

attention while Lindisfarne was the centre of the Northumbrian church. Eddius says that its roof let in water, there were no windows and birds nested in it. Under Wilfrid's restoration the roof ridges were covered with lead, the walls were whitewashed and windows installed. Wilfrid also endowed the church with estates. Although Biscop is said by Bede to have brought over glass makers from Gaul in 675-76 Eddius suggests that Wilfrid had already introduced masons and artisans into Northumbria and they no doubt worked on the York church which was destroyed by fire in 741.

Having restored order in the church Theodore summoned a council or synod at Hertford in 672. Not all bishops attended and Wilfrid sent a representative although the council reflected one English church united in action and, until 735, recognising one archbishop. Theodore aimed (although there was no agreement on this at Hertford) to divide large dioceses including Lichfield and York which were tribal and unmanageable. Lindsey, part of the Lichfield diocese, was annexed to Northumbria by Ecgfrith in 674 and came under the control of York. It was separated from York in 677 and remained independent until retaken by Æthelred of Mercia in 679. As Ecgfrith's kingdom expanded so did Wilfrid's diocese. Not only was a bishop's diocese related to a kingdom but the size of the diocese determined the income of the bishop. Such income whether in cash or kind was used among other things for the building and repair of churches (Wilfrid's restoration at York is an example of this) where the outlay was not covered by monastic endowments. To split a diocese would mean splitting the bishop's income. And Theodore, insisting that Chad travelled on horseback to emphasise episcopal dignity, may also have recognised the difficulties of bishops displaying too much worldliness and wealth, a problem recognised by Gregory the Great. There was also the question of whether proper pastoral care was practical in a large diocese. Both issues were acknowledged by Bede in his letter to Egbert, then bishop of York, and it was quite possible that they were the motives for Theodore's division of Northumbria.

Theodore's ideas about a diocese did not coincide with those of Wilfrid who had been influenced by what he saw in Gaul. Wilfrid however incurred the envy and hate of some and Eddius notes that he made gifts "to the clergy as well as to the laity with such magnificence that his equal could not be found".

Wilfrid's fall was linked to his encouragement of Ecgfrith's queen Æthelthryth to become a nun. Ecgfrith had married Æthelthryth, daughter of Anna king of the East Angles in a political alliance. She had previously been married to Tondberht prince of the South Gyrwas but he died shortly after the wedding. On her marriage to Ecgfrith she was much older than her husband who was fifteen. About 672-3 Æthelthryth granted land at Hexham to Wilfrid. This was Wilfrid's first grant in Bernicia, his existing holdings in Northumbria being in Deira. With Bernician expansion to the north the grant would have been useful giving Wilfrid a foothold in dominant Bernicia. In the prevailing political climate Ecgfrith may have regarded the Hexham grant as a nuisance. Eddius says of Wilfrid's Hexham "nor have we heard of any other house on this side of the Alps built on such a scale". Allowing for Eddius' bias the church of Saint Andrew must have been a considerable achievement. It is described in terms similar to those used of Ripon with their crypts, spiral stairs and walls of considerable height. Below the choir at Hexham are the remains of the apse of Wilfrid's church from which it has been calculated that the maximum height was 165 feet, the width across the transept 126 feet and the nave 70 feet. Hexham was built using stones from the disused Roman site at Corbridge (Ripon may have drawn on nearby Aldborough). Both churches reflect the adoption of the Romanesque style for Wilfrid was clearly impressed by the basilicas of Gaul and Italy.

Æthelthryth did not consummate the twelve year marriage to Ecgfrith, a fact confirmed by Wilfrid to Bede, and Wilfrid was apparently offered land and wealth by Ecgfrith if he could persuade her to do so. Instead she went to Coidingham receiving the veil from Wilfrid. Ecgfrith held Wilfrid responsible for the remainder of his reign. A year after entering Coldingham Æthelthryth went to Ely where she founded a convent and was its first abbess. Her successor was her sister Sexburh who had been the wife of Eorcenberht of Kent. Sixteen years after Æthelthryth's death Sexburh had her body translated into the church. On exhumation her body was found to be incorrupt, evidence of her virginity. Her physician Cynefrith and Wilfrid were witnesses to the exhumation. Cynefrith who had been present at her death said that the incision he had made to drain a tumour in her jaw had healed.

Ecgfrith's second marriage was ecclesiastically valid since Æthelthryth although still alive had taken the veil. His new queen Iurminburh was a bitter enemy of Wilfrid and moved Ecgfrith to jealousy of Wilfrid's "temporal glories", his "riches, the number of his monasteries, the greatness of his buildings, his countless army of followers arranged in royal vestments and arms". Kings had to maintain their authority and not allow themselves to be threatened by overbearing churchmen. Ecgfrith seeing Wilfrid in this way and aggravated by the breakup of his first marriage removed Wilfrid from office, seized his assets and expelled him from Northumbria. It is conceivable that, similarly, Coenwalh of the West Saxons expelled Agilbert and Wulfhere of Mercia expelled Winfrith regarding them as too dominating for comfort. It could also be that apart from dynastic considerations Oswiu may have had something of this in mind when making his decision at the Synod of Whitby.

Theodore, aided says Eddius by Ecgfrith and without Wilfrid's agreement (Wilfrid's proxy must have dissented at Hertford), divided Wilfrid's diocese into three. Bosa from Whitby was consecrated bishop of Deira with his seat at

York while Eata abbot of Lindisfarne became bishop of Bernicia with a choice for his seat at Hexham or Lindisfarne. Eadhæd who had accompanied Chad to Canterbury became bishop of Lindsey. In this division Theodore, as he did elsewhere in England at this time, brought Irish and Roman organisation together with bishops given particular sees with particular seats, (the latter not always where they had been in Roman Britain), and the sees were related to tribal or political boundaries. At the time of the division Wilfrid was politically weak, alienated from king and queen and Alhfrith was no longer on the scene to provide support. Wilfrid left England between February and September 677 to go to Rome to appeal to the pope, the first such appeal by an Englishman. Eddius suggests some initial, but no subsequent, support for Wilfrid's appeal. It should be noted that the bishops appointed in Wilfrid's place were Northumbrian and Wilfrid had no quarrel with them personally. As a result of a storm he was forced to land in Frisia in the winter of 677. In the following spring he went to the court of Dagobert II where he stayed for the remainder of 678. Dagobert offered Wilfrid the bishopric of Strasbourg but Wilfrid declined. With Dagobert's bishop Deodatus as guide Wilfrid then went to the court of the Christian Perctarit, king of the Lombards. Eddius comments that Perctarit had been approached by Wilfrid's opposition at home (in effect Ecgfrith) to detain him but had refused to become involved and allowed Wilfrid to continue his journey to Rome unmolested.

A monk Coenwald had carried correspondence from Theodore to Pope Agatho so the latter was therefore aware of the situation when Wilfrid arrived in Rome. It is likely that Theodore's letter was concerned with matters in the English church rather than with Wilfrid specifically. Wilfrid's appeal was heard by a council of fifty-three bishops in October 679. They sought a middle path so that Wilfrid should be restored to York. The bishops appointed in Wilfrid's place should vacate their seats and be replaced by those chosen by Wilfrid who would be advised by a local council. In other words Theodore's plan to divide the Northumbrian see was reinforced while putting right the division of the see without Wilfrid's approval.

Additionally the pope confirmed Wilfrid's possession of Hexham and Ripon monasteries. The council also discussed the English church with Wilfrid vouching for its orthodoxy. Some difference between Theodore and his bishops, other than that involving Wilfrid but connected to Theodore's policy of expanding the English episcopate, was considered and as a result it was decided that only the archbishop of Canterbury and eleven bishops were needed in England. Wilfrid's appeal may have prompted confirmation rather than expansion of this number.

Wilfrid spent some time in Rome before returning to Northumbria in 680. Eddius gives an account of Wilfrid's return through the Frankish kingdom. Dagobert II had been assassinated and the account does not fit in easily with Wilfrid's delay in Rome. It is an occasion when Wilfrid was confronted by a bishop with a small army and defended himself connecting pilgrimage to service to the nation. Wilfrid "with all humility" presented to a Northumbrian council "the written judgement of the Apostolic See... and subscription of the whole synod ... with its bulls and stamped seals". The Roman council's decision was rejected, Eddius explains, either because it was regarded as unpalatable or because it had been "bought for a price". Wilfrid though was not criticised for appealing to the pope in the first place. This response reflects the limited authority of the pope in Northumbria and lack of respect for a church susceptible to simony.

Ecgfrith and his council had Wilfrid imprisoned for nine months depriving him of everything except his clothes. The queen took Wilfrid's reliquary or vessel containing the chrism or consecrated oil for anointing and wore it as an ornament. Iurminburh's hostility to Wilfrid is pointed up even more by Eddius' account of the visit to Coldingham by Ecgfrith and Iurminburh during a royal progress. Iurminburh became ill diagnosed as possessed by a devil. Æbbe attributed this to Ecgfrith's treatment of Wilfrid. Wilfrid had been imprisoned in solitary confinement at the unidentified royal estate of Broninis under the care of a reeve named Osfrith. Possibly because Ecgfrith found the reeve sympathetic to Wilfrid had him moved to Dunbar, then under English control, whose reeve Tydlin was harsh. One aspect of Wilfrid's imprisonment brought out by Eddius is the light emanating from Wilfrid's dark cell attributed to angelic visitation. The apostle Peter in prison had the same kind of experience and so too had Columba. Wilfrid's experience is put in the same terms as the solace received by the Irish Saints for their trials. During Wilfrid's imprisonment Ecgfrith it seems tried to persuade him to submit to his will rather than that of Rome. Wilfrid's refusal demonstrates his moral as well as physical courage. His release was effected through the agency of Æbbe but while Wilfrid was released he was not restored.

Æbbe's part in Wilfrid's release shows that not all Ecgfrith's family was hostile to him. Æbbe was Oswald's sister. Bede obtained information about miracles attributed to Oswald from Acca and known to Wilfrid. Also the monks at Hexham were actively associated with the cult of Oswald, for example, making annual pilgrimages on the eve of the anniversary of Oswald's death to Heavenfield where they built a commemorative church. If Wilfrid could be linked with the cult of Oswald it could conceivably explain how Wilfrid in dynastic politics gave him favour with Æbbe. Alternatively, Ecgfrith may have bowed to his aunt Æbbe who saw that little could be achieved by Wilfrid's imprisonment.

Theodore did not resist Ecgfrith's will enacted by his council and could not risk alienating the patron of the English church in the north. With Wilfrid exiled, Theodore took the opportunity to make further changes in the organisation of the Northumbrian church in 681. A bishopric was set up at Abercorn, the Picts then being under English rule until 685, and another Bernician bishopric was established at Hexham (in addition to Lindisfarne from then held by Eata). Theodore consecrated Trumwine and Tunberht (previously abbot of Gilling) respectively while Eadhæd bishop of Lindsey who was expelled from Mercia in 679 was appointed bishop of Ripon. Ripon became a bishopric out of expediency and it was only temporary with no further bishops after Eadhæd and Wilfrid.

After his release Wilfrid stayed for a short while among the Middle Angles and West Saxons before settling for five years among the South Saxons. Eddius says that Wilfrid was allowed to stay among the Middle Angles by a reeve named Berhtwold nephew of King Æthelred and was given land on which he founded a monastery which was still there when Eddius wrote. Wilfrid was not safe since Æthelred's queen was Ecgfrith's sister Osthryth. He encountered a similar situation among the West Saxons whose queen was Iurminburh's sister. The South Saxons were the last heathen English although Bede remarks curiously that their king Æthelwealh had been baptised under Wulfhere of Mercia. Wilfrid embarked on a programme of evangelisation and was granted an estate of eighty seven hides by the king at Selsey which became the episcopal seat. Eddius does not tell the story mentioned by Bede that Wilfrid taught the South Saxons to fish using nets at a time of famine. To show that Christianity could reap material benefits was an aspect of conversion complementing conversion by persuasion or royal dictat. In 685 Æthelwealh was killed by Cædwalla. Cædwalla had British connections and sought the throne of the West Saxons (Wessex). With Wilfrid's lack of security in Wessex the possibility of friendship with Cædwalla is not unreasonable. At the same time Wilfrid may have undermined Æthelwealh's position. Bede says Cædwalla was driven out of Wessex although Eddius does not mention this. After finally becoming king of Wessex in 685 Cædwalla took Sussex and the Isle of Wight. While Wilfrid is presented by Eddius as converting Cædwalla Bede does not reflect Cædwalla in a Christian light. Wilfrid confirmed his allegiance to Cædwalla who gave him one quarter of the Isle of Wight as well as many unspecified lands and gifts. Wulfhere of Mercia had conquered the Isle of Wight in 661 and given it to Æthelwealh. Before Wilfrid could convert its heathen inhabitants he was able to return to Northumbria which had a new king Aldfrith and transferred responsibility for the task to his sister's son Beornwine. Wilfrid also appointed a priest Hiddila to assist.

In 686 Theodore and Wilfrid were reconciled. This is not mentioned by Bede and the words attributed to Theodore by Eddius may have been more gushing than was the case. However, nearing the end of his life Theodore regretted that he had co-operated with kings when Wilfrid was deprived of his possessions and proposed to a council of bishops in London that Wilfrid should succeed him. This proposal must have been rejected. Wilfrid did ask that the reconciliation be publicised and that the property confiscated restored. Accordingly Theodore wrote to Aldfrith, Ælfflæd and Æthelred of Mercia. On Wilfrid's return to Northumbria the decision of six years earlier was not implemented and Wilfrid was not restored to his full diocese. Bosa remained at York until his death in 705. Cuthbert had been appointed to Hexham following Tunberht's expulsion either by Theodore for disobedience or because of friction with Ecgfrith who regarded him as an ally of Wilfrid. After Eata's death from dysentery in 686 John became bishop of Hexham the following year until he moved to York in 706. Meanwhile Wilfrid went to Ripon as bishop (Eadhæd presumably having died) only having held Hexham for a year and administering Lindisfarne until a successor to Cuthbert (Eadberht) had been appointed. Between Cuthbert's death and Eadberht's appointment there was some disorder on Lindisfarne in consequence of which a number of monks left. The problems arising during Wilfrid's administration may have been connected with his dislike of the Irish church.

Relations between Aldfrith and Wilfrid were erratic. They deteriorated when, following Theodore's death in 690, Wilfrid renewed his claim to the whole Northumbrian diocese. Aldfrith demanded that Wilfrid conform to what had been done in Theodore's middle years as archbishop. Eddius also mentions that Ripon had been dispossessed of lands and that Wilfrid no longer had control of his see. Wilfrid did not co-operate and was expelled in 691. It is possible that Aldfrith's Irish background may have been a contributory factor in the deteriorating relationship between the two. On this as on the previous occasion of Wilfrid's expulsion Eddius provides an explanation for events whereas Bede reports them without comment. Despite Wilfrid's continuing disputes stable relations between king and church were achieved under Aldfrith.

Wilfrid went to Mercia where he was responsible for the foundation of numerous monasteries. At first he was responsible for the diocese but he later restricted himself to the Middle Angles. He again petitioned the pope (now Sergius I) although he did not actually go to Rome. The pope arranged for a synod to be held in England to hear Wilfrid's petition and this took place, in 702 at Austerfield near Doncaster which strangely Bede does not mention, after a gap of some ten years after Wilfrid's departure for Mercia. This time lapse is not recognized by Eddius who seems to have lacked information. Bede on the other hand knew about Swithberht's consecration in 693 and that Wilfrid had attended Æthelthryth's translation in 695-6. It seems that Wilfrid consecrated Oftfor bishop of the Hwicce about this time. Presumably the pope's decision had been made during the latter part of this period. Berhtwold who had succeeded Theodore in 693 attended the synod together with most of the English bishops as well as Wilfrid. While full details of the synod are not clear, from Eddius' emotive account there was hostility to Wilfrid. The synod was attempting to ascertain whether Wilfrid was prepared to compromise with those present but Eddius has Wilfrid refusing anything contrary to the judgement of Rome. Wilfrid was left with Ripon monastery to which he must confine himself and not exercise the functions of a bishop. Yet Wilfrid could hardly have been given an option which would result in all the Northumbrian bishops being deprived of their office. Wilfrid gave notice of his third appeal to the pope and after leaving his Mercian interests in the hands of Æthelred departed for Rome with a small group of companions including Acca. It seems he travelled from Gaul to Rome on foot. After visiting Willibrord *en route* they were received by Pope John VI. During four months early in 704 Wilfrid asked that Pope Agatho's original judgement should be enforced with the minimum that Hexham and Ripon were restored. His response at the hearing of the papal council to the charge from Berhtwold of resisting the authority of the archbishop and the synod at Austerfield brought by representatives who followed him to Rome was that while refusing unconditional submission he agreed to accept any decision in line with Agatho's original ruling. Eddius says that the pope adjourned the hearing to consult the written representations of opposing parties and the decisions of Agatho and Sergius I.

When the hearing was reconvened both parties had the opportunity to restate their case. Wilfrid said that he would submit to Berhtwold providing this was in accordance with the judgement of Rome. According to Eddius after having successfully gone through seventy sittings of the council (an exaggeration) "the joy of victory" came upon Wilfrid as the council decided to take scrupulous care in sifting all the charges in order to "settle the matter finally". The outcome, however, was that Wilfrid's case had not been furthered. A decision would not be made in the absence at Rome of Wilfrid's actual accusers. The pope instructed Berhtwold to hold a synod in England with Bosa and John present to resolve the matter and the kings of Northumbria and Mercia were reminded of the judgements of Agatho and Sergius. If the synod did not produce the desired result then the issue would have to go to a "fuller council" at Rome. In taking this step Pope John was being very careful since papal authority had been seen to be difficult to maintain in England. At the same time he could not ignore his predecessors and let Wilfrid lose and in bidding Berhtwold hold a synod he was buying time. Eddius adds that while in Rome Wilfrid attended a synod in which he confirmed that the faith in "all the northern part of Britain and Ireland and the islands, which are inhabited by the races of Angles and Britons as well as Scots and Picts" was orthodox.

By this stage Wilfrid had held episcopal office for forty years and was over seventy. He suffered a serious illness, possibly a stroke, on the way back to England. He was taken to Meaux where he had a vision somewhat similar to one experienced by Columba. It was of Saint Michael who told him that he must build a church in honour of the Virgin Mary. (This was built at Hexham near his first church there and only slight remains incorporated into buildings facing Hexham market survive). On recovering Wilfrid asked for Acca to whom he related his vision. (Bede gives his friend Acca a prominent place in his account). Wilfrid and his party then crossed to Kent where representatives of Wilfrid spoke with Berhtwold and a reconciliation was effected. Wilfrid returned to Mercia and showed the papal judgement to Æthelred, now an abbot and ruling as protector to his young nephew Coenred. He then sent messengers to Aldfrith to arrange a meeting but Aldfrith died without anything having been achieved. Eddius says Aldfrith was unco-operative but falling ill vowed that if healed he would "remedy everything in accordance with ... the judgment of the Apostolic See". If he died he enjoined his successor to reach a peaceful settlement with Wilfrid. This was witnessed among others by Ælfflæd and an abbess Æthelburh (Æthelthryth's sister).

After Aldfrith's death a certain Eadwulf seized the throne in a dynastic struggle. Apart from what Eddius records nothing is known of Eadwulf. He was a relative of Aldfrith's (the relationship is not specified) and presumably belonged to one line of the Bernician ruling family. Aldfrith's son Osred was only eight years old at the time and the prospect of his succession would not have guaranteed stability. Wilfrid may have been sympathetic to Eadwulf whose son was at Ripon with Wilfrid but for reasons unknown Eadwulf would not help him. Two months after taking the throne Eadwulf was driven out by Berhtfrith for the Osred faction which had gained the upper hand. Berhtfrith became protector to Osred. Perhaps Wilfrid had become involved in the struggle changing his allegiance to Osred. He was evidently sufficiently thought of to have Osred as his adopted son.

In Osred's first year as king (706) Berhtwold came north to arrange a synod with Osred to resolve Wilfrid's dispute. The king and his chief men (including Berhtfrith described by Eddius as "next in rank to the king"), three bishops, their abbots and Ælfflæd, the "best counsellor of the whole province" met Berhtwold and Wilfrid "near the river Nidd", probably Nidd village. The papal judgement was read out and Berhtfrith asked the archbishop to explain what this meant. The bishops dissented appealing to what had been decided by Theodore and Ecgfrith and between Berhtwold and Aldfrith. Ælfflæd advocated a solution in accordance with Aldfrith's last

71

wishes. After some conferring the synod reached a settlement which meant that at the end of the day Wilfrid had not achieved anything from his appeals to Rome. He was bishop of Hexham which was special to him and he recovered his monasteries at Hexham and Ripon and their revenues but he failed to regain the see of York.

Not long after the synod Wilfrid suffered a recurrence of the same illness which afflicted him on his return from Rome although he again recovered and remained in satisfactory health for a year and a half. Then Wilfrid in the presence of two abbots and eight brothers had the treasures of Ripon, which included gold, silver and precious stones, brought out and instructed the treasurer to divide them into four parts for distribution. One part was to go to the churches of Saint Mary the Virgin and Saint Paul the Apostle at Rome, another to be divided between Hexham and Ripon to purchase the friendship of kings and bishops (Bede makes the point that Aidan would not offer money to influential people), and the last part to go to those who accompanied him in exile. He appointed Acca to succeed him at Hexham, and his kinsman Tatberht, to whom he related his life story, his successor at Ripon. After this Wilfrid went to one of his monastic foundations which Bede says was "in the district of Oundle" and ruled by Abbot Cuthbald. The possibility has been advanced that this was the abbey of Peterborough which was in the province of Oundle. Wilfrid's connection with Peterborough would date from his time as bishop of the Middle Angles. While there he again fell ill and died at the age of seventy-five in 709. The date of death is not known but is traditionally 12 October. His body was brought to Ripon for burial.

Wilfrid's achievement lay in his role in deciding the shape of the church in his day expressed at Austerfield in terms of the elimination of the Irish Easter and tonsure and the introduction to Northumbria of chanting and the rule of Saint Benedict. He brought the Northumbrian church into contact with Rome through his visits there. Wilfrid was an enthusiastic evangelist and defended and maintained the church's authority clearly demonstrating its independence from the ambit of kings (in whose courts he moved with ease) to such an extent that he spent twenty-six out of the forty-six years of his episcopacy in exile. He was ambitious as his large building programmes at Hexham, Ripon and York show and he influenced the art and architecture of the day but he was opposed by those who disliked or resented his wealth and pomp. Wilfrid's outlook had been largely shaped by his travels on the Continent and both the opposition to him and his opposition to Theodore were probably the result of his ideas of what a bishop should be as reflected by the grandiosity of Gaulish bishops. He could be likened to a prince-bishop. Although he sought to maintain the universal authority of the Roman church he operated as an individualist confusing his own interests with those of church order. Yet scarcely had the Northumbrian church been reorganised than further change was hindered by his disputes. Wilfrid probably had an eye to the raising of York to metropolitan status. This however did not occur for a quarter of a century after his death and until then the unity of the English church was preserved.

CHAPTER 9

John of Beverley

THE PRINCIPAL SOURCE FOR BISHOP JOHN is Bede's *Ecclesiastical History*. Unlike Cuthbert or Wilfrid there is no "Life" of John and material provided by Bede and Alcuin who follows Bede amounts to no more than a handful of biographical details and miracle stories. It is almost a miniature version of his *Life of Saint Cuthbert* but without the elaborate reflection and commentary.

John ordained Bede as deacon and priest (about 691 and 702 respectively) and was a much loved man only surpassed in veneration by Cuthbert. A native of Harpham he studied under Archbishop Theodore and Abbot Hadrian at Canterbury and on his return to Yorkshire entered Whitby under Hild. In 687 John was consecrated bishop of Hexham. He was one of five monks of Whitby who became bishops. During Lent and when opportunities arose he would retire with a few companions to read and pray to a retreat one and a half miles from Hexham associated today with Saint John's Lee. As an act of charity he would take some poor or infirm person to stay with him there. In 706 John became bishop of York in succession to Bosa while Wilfrid succeeded to Hexham as part of the resolution of his dispute with the Northumbrian kings. When bishop of York John founded the monastery of Deirawood (Beverley).

Bede records that many miracles were told about John but provides accounts only of five, four of which were described by Berhthun who was John's deacon and in Bede's day abbot of Beverley "a most reverend and truthful" man and one by Herebald abbot of Tynemouth. The first account was not really a miracle. It took place at Lent when John was bishop of Hexham and involved a dumb youth. The story reflects John's concern for the poor and handicapped and presents him as a man with special gifts applied in the church's healing ministry. It also provides the earliest account of a treatment for the dumb and shows John working alongside physicians. As with other miracle stories in the *Ecclesiastical History* the biblical parallels drawn with John are essential to Bede's treatment of him.

There was in a village not far away a dumb youth known to the bishop, who often used to come to him to receive alms and had never been able to utter a single word. Besides this, he had so much scabbiness and scurf on his head that no hair could grow on the crown save for a few rough hairs which stuck out around it. The bishop had this young man brought and ordered a little hut to be built for him in the enclosure of their dwelling, in which he could stay and receive his daily allowance. On the second Sunday in Lent, he ordered the poor man to come in to him and then he told him to put out his tongue and show it him. Thereupon he took him by the chin and made the sign of the holy cross on his tongue; after this he told him to put his tongue in again and say something. 'Say some word,' he said, 'say *gæ*,' which in English is the word of assent and agreement, that is, yes. He said at once what the bishop told him to say, the bonds of his tongue being unloosed. The bishop then added the names of the letters: 'Say A', and he said it. 'Say B', and he said that too. When he had repeated the names of the letters after the bishop, the latter added syllables and words for the youth to repeat after him. When he had repeated them all, one after the other, the bishop taught him to say longer sentences, which he did. After that those who were present relate that he never ceased all that day and night, as long as he could keep awake, to talk and to reveal the secrets of his thoughts and wishes to others which he could never do before. He was like the man who had long been lame, who, when healed by the Apostles Peter and John, stood up, leapt and walked, entering the Temple with them, walking and leaping and praising God, rejoicing to have the use of his feet of which he had so long been deprived. The bishop rejoiced with him at his cure and ordered the physician to undertake to heal his scabby head. He did as he was bidden and, with the help of the bishop's blessing and prayers, his skin was healed and he grew a beautiful head of hair. So the youth gained a clear complexion, ready speech, and beautiful curly hair, whereas he had once been ugly, destitute, and dumb. So rejoicing in his new-found health he returned home, which he preferred to do though the bishop offered him a permanent place in his own household.

When bishop of York John arrived at a convent at Watton near Beverley then ruled by abbess Hereburh Cwenburh her daughter and a nun there was seriously ill. She had been bled in the arm but in consequence was subject to a violent pain which quickly increased so that the arm became so swollen it could barely be encircled with two hands and she could not bend her elbow. The abbess thought that if John blessed or touched her daughter her condition would improve. In this detailed eye witness account of Berhthun's John demonstrates his recollection of some medical instruction received in Kent. He discovers that Cwenburh had been bled on the fourth day of the moon but says it was dangerous to bleed when the light of the moon and the pull of the tide was increasing (he does not say why). After an initial reluctance John said a prayer over her and gave her his blessing. Later, at meal time, Cwenburh called for Berhthun who found that the pain had gone. The swelling was still there but subsided when John and Berhthun left the convent.

In the two miracles which follow John is seen consecrating village churches for the thegns Puch and Addi as part of his episcopal functions. Berhthun is again an eyewitness for the first in which Puch's wife is cured but in this and the following one, in which John heals a serving boy, detail is poor compared with the other three stories about John.

Bede ends his account of John with a tale of horse racing told by its subject Herebald, in his younger days one of John's clergy. It is another occasion on which John works with a medical practitioner. Herebald tells how he and a number of his contemporaries were travelling with John and came to a stretch of level road suitable for racing their horses. At first John refused their request to race but relented with the proviso that Herebald did not participate even though Herebald was confident in the horse John had provided for him. Nevertheless Herebald joined in racing with the others at full speed:

> While the bishop and I were watching, and the horses were galloping back and forth along the course, I was so overcome by a spirit of wantonness that I could hold back no longer; so in spite of his command, I mingled among the contestants and began to race with them. As I did so, I heard him behind my back, saying with a sigh, "Oh, how you grieve me by riding in such a way!" I heard, yet I went on against his orders; immediately, as my fiery horse took a great leap over a hollow in the road, I fell and at once lost all feeling and power of movement just as if I were dead. For in that place there was a stone, level with the ground and covered by a thin layer of turf, and no other stone was to be found over the whole plain. Thus it happened by chance, or rather by divine intervention in order to punish my disobedience, that I hit it with my head and with the hand which I had put under my head as I fell; so my thumb was broken and my skull fractured and, as I said, I lay like a corpse. As I could not be moved, they put up a tent for me to lie in. Now it was about one o'clock in the afternoon and I lay as quiet as if I were dead until evening, when I revived a little and was carried home by my companions. I lay speechless all night, now vomiting blood because some internal organs had been ruptured in my fall. The bishop was deeply grieved by my accident and by the disaster, because he had a special

76

affection for me. So he would not sleep that night with his clergy, as was his custom, but spent the whole night alone in vigil and prayer, imploring, as I suppose, God's mercy for my recovery. In the early morning he came in to me, said a prayer over me, and called me by name. I awoke as though from a heavy sleep and he asked me if I knew who it was who was talking to me. I opened my eyes and said, "Yes, you are my beloved bishop." He answered, "Can you live?" I said, "I can, with the help of your prayers, if it is the Lord's will." Then, placing his hand on my head with words of blessing, he returned to his prayers; when he came back very soon afterwards, he found me sitting up and able to speak; and, urged as it soon appeared by a divine instict, he began to ask me whether I was perfectly certain that I had been baptized. I answered that I knew without any doubt that I had been washed in the fountain of salvation for the remission of sins, and I told him the name of the priest who had baptized me. The bishop answered, "If you were baptized by that priest you were not perfectly baptized, for I know that, when he was ordained priest, he was so slow-witted that he was unable to learn the office of catechism or baptism; and for this reason I ordered him not to presume to exercise this ministry because he could not perform it properly." Saying this, he made it his business to catechize me forthwith; as he did so and breathed upon my face, I immediately felt better. Then he called a doctor and ordered him to set and bind up my fractured skull. As soon as I had received his blessing, I was so much better that on the next day I mounted my horse and journeyed with him to another place; and very soon after I had fully recovered, I was washed in the water of life.

In 718 John retired to his monastery at Beverley his priest having been consecrated as his successor (Wilfrid II). He died on 7 May 721 and was buried there. The remains beneath the commemorative stone in the nave of Beverley Minister are probably those of John.

CHAPTER 10

Willibrord and the
English mission to the Continent

NORTHUMBRIA MADE AN IMPORTANT CONTRIBUTION to missionary work on the
Continent by the English. It was Wilfrid who in preaching to the Frisians in
677-78 set the precedent for the English missions. The Merovingian kingdom
covered most of Gaul and the German countries but not Frisian and Saxon
lands although the frontiers of Frisia varied according to the extent of
Frankish strength. After 639 a succession of minority kings resulted in a series
of power struggles from which eventually emerged the Carolingians under
Pippin II. Roman Christianity had taken hold although papal influence was
very limited because of the extent of control by the king over the church.
With the erosion of royal power the church became territorial with bishops
under the thumb of local aristocratic families to which they could be
related. In consequence ecclesiastical organisation disintegrated. Pockets
of paganism survived with Frankish frontiers and outside these frontiers the
Frisians and the Saxons remained heathen. From 610 the Irish had been
involved in evangelism with Columbanus and Gallus in Switzerland and
Kilianus in Franconia which belonged to the dukes of Thuringia. However
evangelism by the Frankish church had been limited although the work
of Amandus of Aquitaine extended to the Basques and Slavs. Amandus was
bishop of Maastricht in 649 and worked in Antwerp where he built a church
in the castle. Antwerp bordered on but was not part of Frisian territory. At
Utrecht a church had been built before 612 in the old Roman fortress granted
by King Dagobert I to the bishop of Cologne with the condition that he
preached to the Frisians. Following the bishop's failure to do so the pagans
reduced the church to its foundations. Such was the situation in the mid 650s
when Wilfrid visited Gaul on his way to and from Rome.

In the Frankish power struggles the young Merogingian Dagobert II was deposed and exiled to a monastery in Ireland. Later, in 675, Wilfrid was asked for help in securing Dagobert's return when there was another revolt involving Ebroin. Wilfrid responded bringing Dagobert to Northumbria before sending him home. Dagobert was restored to the throne in 676 but murdered in 679. In 677 Wilfrid had been deposed and set out for Rome but had to change his route. In helping to restore Dagobert II he incurred the hostility of Dagobert's enemies, in particular Ebroin, to whom Wilfrid's own opponents seem to have appealed to prevent him reaching Rome. Wilfrid's opponents thought he would sail to Étaples and from there take a direct route to Rome and so sought the help of the Frankish Theodric and Ebroin in waylaying him. Unfortunately bishop Winfrith who had succeeded Chad at Lichfield and who also was travelling to Rome was mistaken for Wilfrid and was captured and robbed and his companions murdered. Instead Wilfrid landed in Frisia and was hospitably received by Aldgisl who resisted Ebroin's attempt to eliminate Wilfrid.

With Aldgisl's agreement Wilfrid evangelised among the Frisians with some but not permanent success. In the spring of 678 Wilfrid left Frisia for the court of the restored Dagobert II and then Rome. When in 702 he went to Rome for the last time Bede says that Wilfrid stayed with Willibrord who had followed Wilfrid's precedent. Eddius does not mention this visit only that Willibrord was working in Frisia in his own lifetime. The occasion reflects Wilfrid's interest in the work he had started twenty-five years earlier. It was on this occasion that Wilfrid and Acca heard of the miracles attributed to Oswald. It was doubtless Willibrord who was responsible for the spread of Oswald's cult abroad.

After Wilfrid it was Egbert who expressed the wish to evangelise. Egbert's self-exile has already been noted. The acceptance by the southern Irish church of Roman practices paved the way for Englishmen of Roman persuasion to visit Ireland for pilgrimage, learning and to live the monastic life and Bede warmly acknowledges the reception of his fellow countrymen in Ireland. The Irish concept of voluntary exile in which salvation could be sought through evangelism was an important motive in missionary work. With the conversion of the English completed by Wilfrid's work among the South Saxons and on the Isle of Wight Egbert, who would not return to England, turned his attention to the Continent reflecting the growing desire to take Christianity to the English homelands. Egbert was prevented from going himself by "divine revelations and interventions" as Bede calls them. Egbert had chosen his companions and preparations for the voyage were complete. One of his companions who had served under Boisil at Melrose told Egbert of a dream in which Boisil had appeared with a message for Egbert that he should go to Iona instead, no doubt a retrospective explanation for his eventual presence there. Egbert did not change his mind even with a second such manifestation. It was only when the ship ready loaded and awaiting a favourable wind suffered storm damage that Egbert abandoned the mission.

One of Egbert's companions the hermit Wihtberht went to Frisia instead. Wihtberht arrived in Frisia but found that Aldgisl who had been helpful to Wilfrid had died. His successor was Radbod. He, and his subjects, had lapsed into heathenism destroying churches and other buildings built by the Franks and refused to co-operate with Wihtberht. After two unproductive years Wihtberht returned to Ireland.

Egbert planned another mission. In 690 he sent a group of twelve monks corresponding to the twelve apostles to Frisia. One of the monks was Willibrord. There is no account of Willibrord comparable to Eddius' biography of Wilfrid and nearly all that is known about Willibrord's mission is provided by Bede in the *Ecclesiastical History* and by Alcuin supplemented by references in the *Life of Saint Boniface* by an English priest named Willibald written from collected material, not first hand experience, not long after Boniface's death in 768 and the correspondence of Boniface himself. Alcuin's *Life* was written half a century after Willibrord's death at the request of Beornred abbot of Echternach monastery and later archbishop of Sens. However the work had a double function given that Alcuin was related to Willibrord. The earliest account of Willibrord was compiled by an Irishman whose name is not known but the work itself disappeared although it is likely that it was used by Alcuin. Alcuin followed Bede's *Life of Cuthbert* with a double work on Willibrord in prose (this had a homily attached to it) and in verse. The latter was intended for scholars but does not provide any additional information. Any accurate assessment of Willibrord's personality is not possible particularly since his own correspondence has not survived.

One contemporary manuscript has survived. It is known as Willibrord's calendar. Now in the National Library in Paris it was written by an Englishman early in the eighth century and is a calendar of saints important to Willibrord notably Oswald, Swithberht, Pope Sergius, the Hewalds and Amandus. A marginal entry was made in it by Willibrord himself at the age of seventy in November 728. He refers to himself as Clemens Willibrordus and records his missionary journey of 690 and consecration in 695.

Willibrord was born in 658 probably on 6 November, not long before the Synod of Whitby, apparently in Deira. His parents were both Christian and his father Wilgisl later became a hermit near the mouth of the Humber. Wilgisl was given land there by the king as a perpetual gift on which he built a church dedicated to Saint Andrew and founded a small religious community. Its location may have been that where Ceolfrith waited for a ship to travel to Gaul in 716. Wilgisl was buried there and Alcuin came to administer it because he inherited it. Typically of hagiography Alcuin draws a parallel with John the Baptist who was born for the salvation of many of devout parents. Willibrord's mother is credited with a heavenly vision at conception.

In his youth Willibrord was placed at Ripon, a Roman establishment under Wilfrid, by his father for education and religious pursuits. Alcuin continuing the biblical allusions says he was surrounded by what was virtuous and likens him to Samuel. He was highly gifted and according to a letter by Boniface received the tonsure at Ripon at the age of fifteen. When he was twenty he went to Ireland. At that time, Wilfrid had been expelled from the see of York and this prompted the voluntary exile of monks sympathetic to him. Willibrord may have left for the same reason. Joining Egbert and Wihtberht in Ireland he stayed there for twelve years. Willibrord would have been influenced by the Irish ideas of pilgrimage and exile and for him these involved participation in the new mission to the Continent.

In 687 Pippin II attacked Radbod to recover Frisian lands. The western part of Frisia had thus been annexed by the time Willibrord arrived in 690. Having arrived at the mouth of the Rhine their destination Utrecht Willibrord and his party went on to Pippin and were favourably received. Under Pippin's protection they began to evangelise. Pippin probably sought to impose Christianity as part of his subjugation of the Frisians. After some success had been achieved Willibrord was sent by Pippin to Rome to obtain additional, and from Willibrord's point of view, necessary, support or authority and advice from Pope Sergius I who as part of the universal church was also head of the Frankish church even if in no more than theory. Willibrord, like Augustine, may have looked for authority for his leadership of the mission. Alcuin is confused about Willibrord's visits to Rome here. Willibrord received the anticipated approval from Sergius (Alcuin provides embellishment saying that the pope had a dream in which an angel told him to receive Willibrord with the highest honours). He brought back various relics and liturgical vessels. In his absence at Rome the Northumbrian Swithberht one of Willibrord's party from Ireland had been chosen as bishop by the other members of the group and sent to England for consecration. He was consecrated in 693 by Wilfrid (in exile in Mercia) since Theodore had died in 690 with no successor in place. On returning Swithberht did not stay in Frisia but went to southern Westphalia to preach among the Boructuars. His mission there came to an abrupt end when the Saxons conquered the area. Swithberht was given land at Kaiserswerth near Düsseldorf by Pippin and his wife Plectrudis where he founded a monastery and remained until his death in 713.

The reason for Swithberht's consecration is unclear. There may have been dissension or he may have held an episcopate with particular responsibility to Willibrord. A further explanation is the extension of missionary work outside

Frisia. This can be considered against the work of two English priests mentioned by Bede, but not Alcuin, both with the name Hewald who had been in exile in Ireland and who either accompanied Willibrord or followed him not long after leaving Ireland. They suffered martyrdom at the hands of the Saxons among whom they worked. Bede says they were distinguished by their hair, one was Hewald the Black, the other Hewald the White. Suspicious of Christianity the Saxons murdered them on 3 October 692, Hewald the White having been killed outright, Hewald the Black tortured to death. Their remains were apparently flung into the Rhine but, it is said, were recovered and interred by Pippin in Saint Cunibert's church in Cologne.

With the lack of success of these evangelistic forays the English missionaries decided to establish a firm base in Frisia under Willibrord's leadership. On his return from Rome Willibrord was given the church in Antwerp castle founded by Amandus. The success of Willibrord's mission meant the need for a structured church organisation. It was the Roman emphasis on canon law, organisation and discipline which ensured long-term success on the Continent particularly with the foundation, later, of monasteries by Boniface. The introduction to the Continent by Willibrord and his successors of Roman systems ensured that the authority of the church of Rome should prevail throughout the Frankish kingdom and with it the elimination of any territorial church. Church and state were thus separated on a permanent basis.

Willibrord was again sent to Rome by Pippin this time for consecration as archbishop of the Frisian people. Willibrord may already have been consecrated bishop by the Frankish church. Whether or not this was so, the occasion reflects the wish for a new church province similar to England with an archbishop who could consecrate suffragan bishops. It also represents the first time there had been co-operation between a Carolingian king and the pope, co-operation which was to have a special and considerable impact on future developments on the Continent.

Pope Sergius consecrated Willibrord in Saint Cecilia's Church, Trastevere, on 21 November 695 the eve of the festival day of the patron of music. Sergius gave Willibrord the name Clement after the saint and martyr whose day fell two days later. The name was not inappropriate given the likely end of missionaries working on the Continent.

Pippin gave Willibrord the fortress at Utrecht where he established his archepiscopal seat. As Augustine had established his mission to the English at Kent so Willibrord based his mission to the Frisians at Utrecht and his metropolitan status constituted the introduction of the English system on the Continent. Like Augustine at Canterbury Willibrord at Utrecht built and dedicated churches to Christ and Saint Martin. Willibrord appointed several bishops from among his original companions some of whom had died by 731 although no names are known and educated native clergy to succeed the English missionaries. He was dependent upon secular support for his work. He did try to evangelise beyond Frankish frontiers but failed to convert the Frisians under Radbod. Their conversion was attempted by Boniface who was martyred by them and they did not adopt Christianity until Charlemagne. Willibrord's mission to the Danes was also abortive. Their king was Ongendus (possibly Ongentheow of the poem *Beowulf*) a particularly savage ruler. Willibrord left taking with him thirty boys whom he had freed and baptised intending them for future missionary work although his plans were premature. Sailing back Willibrord was driven by a storm to Heligoland where he killed some cattle for food. The cattle however were regarded as sacred by the natives who worshipped a god called Fosite. Willibrord escaped the natives' hostile response. There is also limited evidence of involvement over a thirteen year period in Thuringia and northern Franconia. Heden the last duke of Thuringia made grants in both to Willibrord in 704 and again in 717 when his advice was sought over the building of a monastery at Hammelburg.

About 700 Pippin and Plectrudis together with Irmina, abbess of Trier, gave land at Echternach, Luxemburg to Willibrord on which he built his monastery, a place of retreat. The ruling family gave the monastery many possessions although the monastery's ownership was transferred to Pippin by Willibrord. Pippin died in 714 survived by his wife and a grandchild. Widespread revolt followed. Willibrord's work was disrupted until 719 when Charles Martel, Pippin's son by another wife and grandfather of Charlemagne, succeeded and restored control and defeated Radbod.

Willibald mentions that after Radbod's death Boniface (Winfrith) of Wessex went to Frisia and offered his services to Willibrord for three years because of the shortage of missionaries in relation to the task of evangelisation. Willibrord tried to persuade Boniface to be consecrated bishop and remain to help him. Technically there should have been only one bishop in each diocese but this type of arrangement was occasionally made and was used by Boniface. In one of his letters Boniface refers to Willibrord's appointment, in old age, of an assistant bishop or *chorepiscopus*. While unusual the precedent for this lay in the East not the bishops of Irish monasticism. The concept was acknowledged in Isidore of Seville's *Ecclesiastical Offices* which was known in Northumbria. Willibrord's appointment set the precedent in the West. Meanwhile, Boniface declined Willibrord's suggestion on the grounds that he was unworthy, too young and well below the canonical age. Boniface felt that he ought to evangelise in the lands to which he had been called by Pope Gregory II and in doing so extended the missionary work on the Continent initiated by Wilfrid and Willibrord. Northumbria and Wessex were thereby to lead not only in the field of learning but in evangelism abroad as well.

Alcuin's *Life* does not end with an account of Willibrord's death but, inevitable in a work of hagiography, provides a substantial section in which he concerns himself with the miraculous. There are nine stories about Willibrord himself followed by accounts of miracles connected with Pippin the Short, son of Charles Martel, whom Willibrord baptised. Pippin the Short was an illustrious warrior who promoted Christianity. Some miracles associated with Willibrord are with those related of other saints biblically inspired although locations and dates are not always fully given. In four stories there is a shortage of wine or spring water which is rectified, allusions to Christ's miracle at Cana. In one such act at Echternach, Willibrord forbade the steward to tell anyone about the miracle until he was dead. Although this is an obvious allusion to Christ's injunction to his disciples to keep his transfiguration secret it resembles one told of Cuthbert and had a similar purpose. Another tells how at Walcheren Willibrord smashed a pagan idol which may have a basis in fact. Willibrord was struck on the head by the idol's custodian with a sword but luckily survived. The custodian died three days later possessed by a devil. Finally in the only miracle involving a cure, Willibrord healed nuns during a plague at a convent, probably Saint Marien-ad-Martyres where Willibrord's portable altar is preserved.

Willibrord survived Bede by four years. Writing in 731 Bede says Willibrord "is still alive and honoured for his great age" and that he had been a bishop for thirty-six years. Willibrord died at the age of eighty-one on 7 November 739 at Echternach and was buried there.

CHAPTER 11

Northumbrian monasticism

THE MONASTIC MOVEMENT IN NORTHUMBRIA got underway during Aidan's episcopate. Monasticism was not part of Augustine's programme of conversion. He established only one monastery during his mission, that of Saint Peter at Canterbury, and there is nothing to indicate that Paulinus intended his own mission to be any different. What Aidan introduced to Northumbria was similar to the system he was familiar with on Iona. Monasteries were regarded as vital to the existence of the church but at the same time it is not to be supposed that their development in Northumbria, or anywhere else in England for that matter, was the result of specific policies of, or wholly controlled by, the ecclesiastical hierarchy.

Usually monasteries were of royal or aristocratic foundation. Families could, however, set up monasteries although this led to the growth of spurious monasteries. Bede expressed his concern about these in a letter, his last known written work, to a former pupil Egbert, bishop of York from 732 and first archbishop of York from 735. Bede had visited Egbert in 733 and hoped to see him again in the following year but being too unwell to travel wrote instead (on 5 November 734). In founding monasteries family lands could be secured by royal charter on a hereditary basis in perpetuity thereby avoiding taxation. Losing control of royal estates and exemptions from dues particularly where monasteries were concerned came to restrict the ability of kings to provide rewards to their supporters. Military service could also be avoided thus putting the defence of the kingdom at risk.

While the roots of western monasticism lay in North Africa, the Egyptian desert and Palestine, continental influences were important in the development of Northumbrian monasteries. The twin Wearmouth-Jarrow for example looked to the monasteries of the lower Rhône valley and Lérins. Lérins was founded by Honoratus (later bishop of Arles) in 410 on a desolate, uninhabited island in the Bay of Cannes. Augustine visited it on his way to England and Biscop spent two years there. Two monasteries were founded near Marseilles by the monk John Cassian who had experience of the Middle East. These monasteries were places of retreat and rigorous asceticism yet, unlike those of the Egyptian desert, were also close by a particularly cultured region where a classical or humanist education could be obtained. Lérins began to provide education comparable with that of its neighbouring region, producing men of high intellectual ability. Many Irish monks are known to have visited Lérins which in turn may have had an important influence on Irish monasteries. Inspired by Gaulish monasteries Biscop was determined that his own foundation would become a centre of learning not an ascetic retreat.

Another continental feature discernible in Northumbria was the Benedictine Rule. This had already been introduced elsewhere in England although not by Wilfrid. It was formulated in Italy by Benedict of Nursia after whom it is named. There were many rules and often monastic founders composed their own. It was not the rule at Canterbury or at Wearmouth-Jarrow. There Biscop's rule was a composite of all that he found best out of seventeen of the oldest rules he had come across and that at Lérins was probably one of them. When compiling it Benedict may have taken a sideways glance at the *Libellus Responsionum* in which Gregory recommended that Augustine should adopt those practices of the Roman and Gaulish churches which seemed best suited to the needs of the English church. Biscop's attitude towards a successor at Wearmouth-Jarrow does show that one part of the Benedictine Rule was advocated there.

The anonymous *Life of Cuthbert* tells how Cuthbert introduced his own rule at Lindisfarne when given responsibility for tightening up discipline. It is difficult to say which rule was already in use there. Some historians have suggested it was the rule of Columbanus and that, with the links between them, this was also observed at Melrose and, initially, Ripon. Cuthbert's rule apparently was followed at Lindisfarne with the Benedictine Rule. If, again, the use of the Benedictine Rule was limited it was, not surprisingly, at Wilfrid's own foundations that the rule was wholly or substantially observed.

Lindisfarne's location was, like that of Lérins, remote. The actual site of Aidan's monastery cannot be identified with certainty. It was not on that of the present priory ruins but possibly on the Heugh with the priory built over the original cemetery only. It lacked the grandeur of the foundations of Wilfrid and Biscop with their churches built in stone. An episcopal church had been built by Finan of hewn oak thatched with reeds (Eadberht later covered the roof and walls with lead) although the interior would have been more sophisticated than the exterior. Lindisfarne was one of a group of Northumbria's earliest monasteries, all Irish foundations for which Oswald gave estates and possessions, which included Melrose, Coldingham, Tynemouth and Gateshead. The latter two receive only a passing reference by Bede in connection with accounts of the miraculous. There was also an early monastery near the mouth of the Tyne on the south side, presumably South Shields, originally occupied by monks but by about 687 inhabited by nuns whose abbess was Verca.

Like Lérins also, Lindisfarne reflected the love of scholarship which manifested itself in other Northumbrian monasteries, if not to the level of Wearmouth-Jarrow. Such a preoccupation was not in evidence among the Roman missionaries of 597 and 601. Something of the calibre of the Lindisfarne monks can be seen in the *Lindisfarne Gospels* intended to be placed near Cuthbert's shrine built after the elevation of 698 and belonging to a small group of Northumbrian manuscripts surviving from the late seventh and early eighth centuries. A tenth century colophon added by the priest Aldred names those involved in their production. They were written by Eadfrith successor to Eadberht as bishop of Lindisfarne at the latter's death on 6 May 698. It has been suggested that Eadfrith did not write the *Gospels* himself rather that they were produced under his direction. Nevertheless the text is the work of one person who was almost certainly also responsible for the decoration. Eadfrith had studied in Ireland and it was there in all likelihood that he developed his abilities as a scribe and illustrator. Simeon of Durham reinforces the attribution to Eadfrith personally. While it is not clear whether Eadfrith was a monk or bishop at the time opinion is that the *Gospels* were written prior to 698.

Scarcely anything is known about Eadfrith's twenty-three year episcopate. In or soon after 699 Eadfrith repaired Cuthbert's oratory on Farne which had become delapidated. After Cuthbert Farne was occupied by the hermit Æthelwold until he died twelve years later. Æthelwold had been a monk at Ripon. During Aldfrith's reign Guthfrith visited Æthelwold on Farne with two other monks. Through Æthelwold's prayers they escaped shipwreck on the homeward journey. Æthelwold was succeeded on Farne by Felgild who was alive and over seventy years of age when Bede wrote his *Life of Cuthbert* and it was during Felgild's occupancy that the repairs were carried out by Eadfrith. In Osred's reign Eadfrith was consulted by one Eanmund about the foundation of a monastery and provided a priest to establish a rule and instruct the brothers.

Aldred says that the *Gospels* were bound by Æthelwold. This was not the hermit but Eadfrith's successor as bishop in 721. After Cuthbert's elevation Æthelwold transferred to Melrose where he was prior and abbot. The last named by Aldred is Billfrith, an anchorite and priest, apparently commissioned by Æthelwold when bishop for the metalwork and gems of the binding. Sadly the binding has not survived.

The *Lindisfarne Gospels* display Mediterranean, Irish and Germanic influences. Textually they are similar to the *Codex Amiatinus* and *Gospel of Saint John* found in Cuthbert's coffin (often referred to as the *Stonyhurst Gospel*), both emanating from the Wearmouth-Jarrow scriptorium, since all use the Vulgate. The *Gospels* and *Codex* evince a method of punctuation advocated by Cassiodorus after Jerome. Cassiodorus' works were known in Northumbria for Bede made extensive use of his biblical commentaries and a bible known as the *Codex Grandior* which came from the library of Cassiodorus' monastery at Vivarium.

Contemporary with the *Lindisfarne Gospels* are the *Durham Gospels*, now at Durham Cathedral, also apparently written at Lindisfarne. The scribe to whom the latter are attributed was also responsible for the *Echternach Gospels* in Paris. Echternach monastery was founded not long after Cuthbert's elevation and about the same time as the production of these manuscripts. Willibrord is known to have kept in touch with Northumbria and it is not improbable that the member of his *familia* visiting Lindisfarne took the *Echternach Gospels* back with him as a gift for Willibrord's new monastery.

No manuscripts have survived from either of Wilfrid's two Northumbrian monasteries, Ripon and Hexham. These were the centres of Wilfrid's monastic network which reflected Irish, Gaulish and Roman influences. Wilfrid was not known as a collector of books and neither Ripon nor Hexham had any particular distinction in learning. In this respect Wilfrid and Biscop were very different and they thus illustrate the importance of the direction given to a monastery by the founder. Hexham's reputation grew under Acca. Bede, a friend of Acca to whom a number of his biblical commentaries were dedicated, described him as a man of great energy who greatly beautified and enlarged his church. He obtained relics of saints and built altars for their veneration. In particular Acca built up a fine library. He invited a famous singer, Maban from Kent to teach his clergy and himself. Maban had been trained by Augustine's successors and stayed in Northumbria for twelve years. He taught new music and restored music which had become imperfect through lapse of time or neglect. Acca is himself described as a singer of great experience. Trained from boyhood under Bosa, Acca became Wilfrid's protegé and eventually abbot and bishop of Hexham. Acca held his see until 732 when for unrecorded reasons he was expelled and replaced by Frithuberht (who was not consecrated until 8 September 734). This was coincidental with an attempt to depose King Ceolwulf the dedicatee of Bede's *Ecclesiastical History*. If Acca was sympathetic to Ceolwulf his deposition may have been the consequence of an allegiance to a king whose position was so weak that on regaining the throne was not strong enough to restore his bishop. Acca lived until 740 and was buried at Hexham. Apparently his grave, in which a portable altar was found (as for Cuthbert and Willibrord), was marked by two great crosses but it has been argued that one of them could have belonged to an adjacent grave.

It was during Aidan's episcopate that women began to participate in the religious life of Northumbria. Bede says that the first woman in Northumbria to become a nun was Heiu. She must have been of noble birth for she founded the monastery at Hartlepool about 640 but left not long afterwards to settle at what might have been Tadcaster. Her successor at Hartlepool was Hild, Edwin's great-niece. Presumably her grandfather was Edwin's brother but the sources do not give more specific information about the relationship. After her baptism by Paulinus Hild engaged in secular occupations for some twenty years. She was in exile following Edwin's downfall but apart from that nothing is known about her early life. That she had been married cannot be ruled out. When she was thirty-three years of age she went to her relatives at the East Anglian court with the intention of going, as an exile, on to Chelles where her sister Hereswith, mother of Ealdwulf king of the East Angles, was already a nun. However, in 648 Hild was recalled to Northumbria by Aidan. She was granted a hide of land on the north bank of the river Wear where with a small group of companions she lived the monastic life for a year. Then came her appointment at Hartlepool. Two nuns from this monastery Hildegyth and Hildethryth mentioned in the *Liber Vitæ* are commemorated by carved stones but it is not known exactly when they lived. With the exception of these scraps of information Hartlepool's history is obscure. In 657 with a grant of ten hides Hild founded the monastery at Whitby then called Streanæshalch. No firm conclusions have been drawn about its Old English etymology. Whitby was one of twelve small votive endowments each of ten hides made available by Oswiu after his victory of 655, six in Bernicia, six in Deira. There is no mention of any further endowments to Whitby although the initial grant was probably augmented. Most Northumbrian monasteries were sited on the coast, as was Whitby, or close by rivers or at river mouths. Good harbours enabled contact with other parts of England and the Continent as well as with other monasteries.

Hartlepool and Whitby were both double houses. The former was probably Northumbria's first and while it is not certain it was a double house under Heiu it was under Hild. This type of foundation was adopted from northern Gaul. It originated with the Eastern monks who responded to women's needs for the monastic life. Eastern monasteries were ruled by abbots. In Gaul nunneries were founded by aristocratic women on their own lands. Attached to them were communities of monks who would say mass and undertake the administrative and manual work the women could not do. The double houses were ruled by abbesses as were their English counterparts and segregation was strictly enforced.

Double houses were also evident to some extent in Spain. Leander, bishop of Seville, compiled a rule for women in monastic life and advocated strict segregation between the two. Leander's brother was Isidore, also bishop of Seville, and at the monastery of Seville were books some of which were by Gaulish authors, including one who had been a monk at Lérins. Another Spanish rule was compiled by Fructuosus who was something of a hermit in the manner of Cuthbert and who travelled on foot like Aidan and Martin of Tours. Fructuosus founded a number of monasteries including one at Cadiz which had a large number of monks. Problems were encountered there similar to those mentioned in Bede's letter to Egbert. Fructuosus voiced concern about the number of spurious monasteries and that so many were becoming monks that, with a reduction in the number of men available for military service, security was threatened. After his death (about 660) the Spanish government tried to limit the number becoming monks. While Fructuosus probably did not found any double houses himself his rule demanded strict segregation within the context of a double house in which the monks were ruled by an abbot and the nuns by an abbess.

In northern Gaul monasticism developed through the work of the Irish missionaries although they did not necessarily have a preference for double houses. The monastery at Luxeuil was founded by Columbanus active at about the time of Augustine's mission to England. About 625 the first nunnery was founded at Remiremont. Bede says that from the mid-seventh century many English went to Gaul for the monastic life and their daughters were sent there to be educated. He names nunneries in northern Gaul with which English women were associated. Faremôutiers-en-Brie was founded by the abbot of Luxeuil and originally a nunnery it became a double house. An Englishwoman Balthild, who had been sold as a slave and became wife of Clovis II was a patron of Chelles near Paris. Given the Irish influence in northern Gaul the Rule of Columbanus was adopted by the majority of women's establishments there. It was known in Northumbria and the possibility of its use at Lindisfarne was mentioned above. The rule at Hartlepool was presumably derived from the one in use at Lindisfarne and in turn observed, together with Irish practices including the Irish Easter, at Whitby by Hild.

The only hint of scandal in any of Northumbria's known double houses was at Coldingham. This may have been sited at Saint Abb's Head named after its abbess Æbbe as was Ebchester in County Durham, a Roman town where she was granted land for a monastery. Neither the details of Coldingham's foundation nor Æbbe's life following her return from exile are known. She could have been a royal widow. Coldingham suffered a fire according to Bede through carelessness although he goes on to attribute it to the wickedness of its members. Using information supplied by a fellow priest Eadgisl, a member of Coldingham at the time but transferred to Wearmouth-Jarrow when most of the community had left the ruined building, Bede tells of Adomnan an Irish monk at Coldingham. In his youth Adomnan had committed some crime and in atonement lived an austere life. He had a premonition of the fire and told Æbbe about it. The community began to improve its ways but relapsed after Æbbe's death so that sudden destruction fell upon the monastery. The *Anglo-Saxon Chronicle* dates the fire to 679. Bede puts it after Æbbe's death. She was alive in 681 and died about 683. The scandal was used to explain the fire yet the evidence of scandal is not entirely consistent. Cuthbert visited Coldingham when at Melrose but neither of the *Lives* points to any impropriety at the time. It is Simeon of Durham who mentions that Cuthbert on visiting Coldingham expressed concern at the behaviour of its occupants and in consequence decided not to allow women at his own monastery at Lindisfarne. The episode suggests a lack of control by Æbbe. The inference is that she ruled it well enough for most of her career and conduct began to deteriorate during her last years. But its reputation could not have been bad for Æthelthryth to have entered it when she did. Bede on the other hand, writing nearly half a century after the event, used eyewitness testimony.

Whitby's achievements under Hild and her immediate successors were considerable. Her foundation was in contact with the churches of Gaul and Germany and Bede refers to the importance of biblical study although the Whitby library was unlikely to have equalled those at Lindisfarne and Wearmouth-Jarrow. No less than five men from Whitby became bishops — Bosa, Ætla (Dorchester), John and Wilfrid II. Oftfor had previously studied at Hartlepool and went on to study in Kent under Archbishop Theodore. Apart from Oftfor, Wilfrid, Ceolfrith and Biscop had been in Kent and Eddius and Maban were brought from Kent. Kentish influences therefore had an important place in the development of Northumbrian monasticism. Oftfor travelled to Rome and on his return to England went to the West Saxons among whom he evangelized and replaced Bishop Bosel who had retired because of ill health. About 692 he was consecrated bishop by Wilfrid, then with the Middle Angles, Theodore having died. Another of Hild's monks Tatfrith ought to have succeeded Bosel but died before he could be consecrated.

Cædmon, for whom there is no independent evidence, is singled out by Bede for special attention. Of British descent Cædmon had followed a secular occupation on the monastery grounds until late in life. He had not previously shown any talent for poetry since at feasts while guests in turn would be asked to sing and entertain Cædmon would leave if the harp was likely to be passed to him. After retiring on one occasion Cædmon dreamt God asked him to sing of the Creation. Bede provides part of Cædmon's song to convey the sense if not the actual words:

Praise we the Fashioner now of Heaven's fabric,
The majesty of his might and his mind's wisdom,
Work of the world-warden, worker of all wonders,
How he the Lord of Glory everlasting,
Wrought first for the race of men Heaven as a rooftree,
Then made he Middle Earth to be their mansion.

Hild heard of Cædmon through the reeve and advised him to enter her monastery. She soon recognised his gift as a useful medium for communicating, in the accepted tradition of the minstrel, the Christian message to the illiterate and unconverted. Bede tells how Cædmon would quickly turn any passage of scripture which was explained to him into delightful and moving poetry in the vernacular and that he never produced frivolous or profane verse. His poetry included Israel's exodus from Egypt, Jesus' incarnation, passion, resurrection and ascension, Pentecost and the terrors of the Last Judgement. If any of Cædmon's work was written down it has not survived. Cædmon died in his sleep in the monastery's infirmary sometime in 680.

Hild apparently suffered from rheumatism during the last six years of her life although she persevered with her duties as abbess until her death at the age of sixty-six on 17 November 680. Bede relates a vision of Hild's soul ascending to heaven by Begu a nun of thirty years' standing at Hackness. Hackness was founded earlier that year by Hild as a cell of Whitby with Frigyth as abbess. A stone found there commemorates Æthelburh another nun listed in the *Liber Vitæ*. Hild was not the subject of a cult and no posthumous miracles were attributed to her. Oddly while her successors were listed in the *Liber Vitæ* Hild was not. She was held in high esteem and this was not affected by her opposition to Wilfrid when he appealed to Rome in 679. Aidan and others who had "loved her heartily for her innate wisdom" would visit her when she was at Hartlepool. Bede adds that "not only ordinary people, but kings and princes" would come and ask her advice and sums up the admiration for her by saying that "all who knew Hild ... used to call her mother".

Eanflæd who had entered Whitby after Oswiu's death in 670 and her daughter Ælfflæd aged twenty-six succeeded Hild ruling as joint abbesses. Whitby was therefore one of those monasteries which Biscop considered in danger of becoming a family possession. Ælfflæd was offered to God as a consecrated virgin as part of Oswiu's vow of 655 and placed with Hild at Hartlepool. She transferred to Whitby on its foundation. After 685 Trumwine who had evacuated from Abercorn assisted in Whitby's administration. In Ælfflæd's time the stress on learning by Hild was maintained. Under her the anonymous *Life of Gregory the Great* was written. The text of one letter written about 700 by Ælfflæd herself survives. It was an introduction for an abbess friend on a pilgrimage addressed to an Adola abbess of a house near

Trier and shows the influence of Aldhelm. Whitby is the only Northumbrian double house from which any text survives but there is no way of knowing whether its nuns worked in the scriptorium. Being an abbess did not prevent Ælfflæd from participating in political affairs. She consulted Cuthbert about her brother's successor and was later involved in securing Osred's accession. She was a supporter of Wilfrid and instrumental in the settlement of 706.

Eanflæd is thought to have died about 704 (although 685 has been offered as an alternative date) and Ælfflæd in 713 or 714 at the age of fifty-nine. An inscribed stone discovered during the excavations at Whitby in 1924-5 almost certainly commemorates Ælfflæd. Her successor's name is not recorded. Oswiu was buried at Whitby as well as its abbesses and other members of the royal family. It is not Bede but the author of the *Life of Gregory the Great* who explains how Edwin's remains (the head excepted which Bede states was at York) were translated to Whitby while Eanflæd was alive. Oswald's relics were at Bardney but to have a rival cult Whitby needed Edwin's remains. Both Oswald and Edwin were regarded as martyrs with Penda as a common enemy. A monk called Trimma from somewhere south of the Humber but a stranger to Lindsey had a recurring dream in which a man told him of a place he should go to (a ceorl Teoful would direct him to the exact spot) and recover Edwin's remains. Trimma initially took no action but the third time he had the dream he proceeded as instructed. The remains were interred in Saint Peter's Church at Whitby.

CHAPTER 12

Wearmouth-Jarrow

WEARMOUTH WAS FOUNDED IN 673 OR 674 with a grant by King Ecgfrith of seventy hides of land to Benedict Biscop. Biscop was a Northumbrian nobleman born in 628. Eddius refers to him as Biscop Baducing, the name Benedict being adopted on entering religious life. Biscop comes from the Latin *episcopus* and its use was not unique. In his earlier years he would have been aware of the Irish form of Christianity as well as the Roman practised by Eanflæd. He was a thegn of King Oswiu who granted him estates in accordance with his rank. At the age of twenty-five he went on a pilgrimage to Rome (653) returning there five times over the following thirty years. On his first visit he was accompanied part of the way by Wilfrid. While Wilfrid delayed in Lyons Biscop went on to Rome completing the journey by sea.

On his second visit he was to have been accompanied by King Alhfrith but the latter's intentions were thwarted by Oswiu so Biscop went on his own. At this time Vitalian was pope. Biscop then went to Lérins where he took the tonsure and his monastic vows and remained for two years. Joining a ship passing through Lérins Biscop returned to Rome intending to stay there permanently. About the same time as his arrival Wigheard came to Rome for consecration as archbishop of Canterbury but died before consecration. At the pope's request Biscop escorted Theodore and Hadrian to England. His second and third visits are dated to 664-68 and Biscop must therefore have been absent from Northumbria at the time of the Synod of Whitby.

Theodore's party travelled to England first by sea to Marseilles and then to Arles where they were delayed seeking Ebroin's permission to continue their journey and as a result of a bad winter. While the activities of Theodore and Hadrian during the winter of 668-69 are documented those of Biscop are not. King Egberht of Kent sent out an ambassador to escort them to England. Bede's accounts in the *Ecclesiastical History* and *Lives of the Abbots of Wearmouth* (the latter written sometime after 716) of the final part of the journey to England and what Biscop did on his return differ. This may reflect inconsistencies between information Bede received from Canterbury and Biscop's own account. Bede says that Biscop became abbot of Saint Peter's Canterbury but Canterbury tradition does not.

Biscop left Canterbury in 671 for his fourth visit to Rome but on this occasion he was motivated not by faith but the desire to acquire books. Not only did he obtain books in Italy but on travelling in the Rhône valley he arranged for others to purchase them for him which he collected at Vienne on the way back. These books provided the core of the library at Wearmouth-Jarrow. Bede drew upon this extensively, for it is unlikely that he travelled to any other library and no further than York or Lindisfarne.

By this time Biscop was in his forties. Back in England he went to the West Saxons. He was a friend of Coenwalh and may have looked to the king for a grant of land on which to found a monastery but by then Coenwalh had died. Oswiu had died in 670 and Ecgfrith was on the throne when Biscop returned home. Wilfrid was then in Northumbria and restoring the church at York and building at Ripon.

At the time of Wearmouth's foundation Biscop was not in good health. He acquired the help of Ceolfrith another Northumbrian nobleman who had taken up monastic life. Ceolfrith was born about 642 and about 660 entered Gilling founded by Oswiu at the behest of Eanflæd in expiation for the murder of her kinsman Oswine. On entry his brother Cynefrith was the monastery's second abbot. Its first was Trumwine an Englishman and kinsman of Oswiu trained and ordained by the Irish. The *Life of Ceolfrith*, the work of an unnamed monk of Jarrow used by Bede, says that Cynefrith left to study in Ireland and was succeeded by their relative Tunberht, later bishop of Hexham. Gilling's existence was short-lived for after the plague of 664 the monks transferred to Ripon at Wilfrid's invitation and the place was abandoned. The transfer provides a hint that although founded when the Irish church dominated in Northumbria Gilling was Roman in its ways. It was a specifically Deiran monastery, the product of dynastic rivalries between Bernicia and Deira and its practices whether Irish or Roman were less important to Eanflæd than concern for her family and the wrong done by a king of the Bernician dynasty.

With his transfer Ceolfrith witnessed the building of Wilfrid's monastery and the introduction of singing and the Benedictine rule. Ceolfrith was ordained priest by Wilfrid about 670 and left not long afterwards with Wilfrid's approval to extend his experience of monastic life. He went to Kent where he probably came into contact with Theodore and Biscop who had recently returned from Rome. Before returning to Ripon Ceolfrith went to Icanho monastery near Aldeburgh whose abbot was Botulph. Once in

Northumbria Biscop invited him to Wearmouth as prior. Ceolfrith may have been attracted by the opportunity for learning at Wearmouth which was not available, or not available to the same extent, at Ripon. From Biscop's point of view Ceolfrith was an ordained priest (and could thus discharge the services at the altar) with useful monastic experience behind him.

The domestic buildings at Wearmouth were constructed in 674. Initially there was a small community of tonsured monks some of whom like Biscop and Ceolfrith were of noble birth. Living and sleeping quarters were built in wood while the church was built in stone after the churches Biscop had seen in Italy and Gaul. For the purpose of building his church Biscop visited Gaul to arrange with a friend, an Englishman Abbot Torthelm whose monastery cannot be identified, for master builders and stone masons to come to Northumbria. While Biscop was in Gaul in 674 Ceolfrith was faced with a dispute with his monks who being of noble birth would not submit to his authority and he returned to Ripon. It is conceivable that they were Bernicians objecting to the authority of a man from Deira. It is also possible there may have been the threat of interference from Biscop's brother who had not taken up the monastic life. After Biscop had returned he visited Ceolfrith at Ripon and persuaded him to go back to Wearmouth. Work on the church which was dedicated to Saint Peter had commenced by 675. Within a year if not complete it had a roof on it and mass was celebrated in it. Benedict then proceeded to bring from Gaul, through messengers, glass makers for the lattice work in the windows, chapels and upper storeys of the church. They taught their craft to the English enabling them to produce glass lamps and cups. Benedict sent to the Continent for vestments, plate and vessels for the altar. The glass and crafts at Wearmouth went against the asceticism of Irish monasteries.

About 678 Biscop accompanied by Ceolfrith set out for Rome for the fifth time. Biscop gave his relative Eosterwine responsibility for the monastery until their return probably in 679. For safety reasons they travelled with a group of armed men as Wilfrid had done. They were received in Rome by Pope Agatho who gave them a letter of privilege which provided for the election of Wearmouth's abbots on the basis of merit not hereditary right. The letter was publicly confirmed by Ecgfrith and the bishops in a synod in 679. It provided immunity from outside interference and although the monastery and its abbots enjoyed harmonious relations with the king Bede was conscious of and was reminding his readers of Wilfrid's problems of the same period.

Significantly through Biscop's journeys to Rome, his monasteries had closer relations with Rome than previously was the case with any English monastery. Biscop and Ceolfrith returned with Abbot John archcantor of Saint Peter's in Rome to teach the monks the singing practised there. He was able to check for Pope Agatho on the orthodoxy of the English church. In this role he presented to the synod at Hatfield the decrees of the Lateran Council of 649. John set off for Rome with a clean bill of health but died *en route*. Nevertheless the copy of the synod's proceedings were taken on to Rome by his companions. John of course was not the first singing teacher in Northumbria for he had as predecessors James the Deacon, Æddi and Æona. John also taught the monks the art of reading aloud and provided a manual of what was required for the festivals for the church year. He instructed many singers who came to him from most of the Northumbrian monasteries. Much of what John had written (music would not have been notational) was available to Bede when writing his *Lives of the Abbots*. Apart from Abbot John, Biscop and Ceolfrith brought back an immense number of books and unspecified relics together with pictures for Wearmouth for instruction, which even the humble and unlettered could understand. The *Life of Ceolfrith* says that they depicted scenes from the Gospels and *Revelation* and representations of Christ, the Virgin Mary and the Apostles. It was not long after Biscop's return that Bede was placed for education at the age of seven at Wearmouth. He was English and born in 672-3 probably on estates on which Wearmouth was to be built. Nothing is known of his family although since he was placed by kinsmen his parents presumably were dead. There is nothing to suggest he was of noble birth.

Following the success of Wearmouth Ecgfrith granted a further forty hides for the foundation of the monastery of Jarrow. The *Life of Ceolfrith* records that twenty-two monks moved with Ceolfrith as their abbot from Wearmouth to Jarrow although only ten of them were tonsured. Bede says there were seventeen monks and he himself, then aged nine or ten, was probably one of the group. The church was dedicated to Saint Paul on 23 April 685 and since the dedication stone at Jarrow (which is still there) places this in the fifteenth year of Ecgfrith and fourth of Abbot Ceolfrith the monastery was probably begun in 681. (The *Life of Ceolfrith* dates Jarrow's endowment to eight years after the beginning of Wearmouth). Bede refers to the monasteries as Wearmouth-Jarrow, although in the first years Biscop was abbot of Wearmouth, Ceolfrith abbot of Jarrow. Then from 681 Biscop appointed a relative Eosterwine abbot of Wearmouth. Although there were three abbots in post at this point, Eosterwine had been appointed because of Biscop's frequent presence at court with insufficient time available for administration. Moreover Biscop was about to set out in 684 (just before Ecgfrith's death) on a sixth, and final, visit to Rome. Eosterwine was born in 650 and was a founder member of Wearmouth. As with Biscop he was in secular life until the age of twenty-four. He was ordained priest in 679. Bede's account of scholarship at Jarrow is balanced by Eosterwine's involvement in the daily round of tasks including winnowing, gardening and baking.

The year after its dedication Jarrow was struck by the plague mentioned in the *Life of Ceolfrith*.

... in the monastery over which Ceolfrith presided all those brethren who could read or preach or recite the antiphons and responds were taken away, with the exception of the abbot and one little lad, who had been reared and taught by him, and who is at this day still in the same monastery, where he holds the rank of priest, and both by written and spoken words justly commends his teacher's praiseworthy acts to all who desire to know of them ...

It is generally accepted that the boy was Bede.

Eosterwine was one of the plague's victims, dying on 6 March 686 at the age of thirty-six, and Sigfrith a deacon of Wearmouth was elected as his successor (Biscop was still on the Continent). Biscop returned later in the year bringing back more books and pictures. In the context of the latter Bede mentions that a second church had been built at Wearmouth dedicated to the Virgin Mary. Biscop also brought back two exceptionally fine silk cloaks which he gave to King Aldfrith in exchange for three hides of land on the Wear's south bank.

Adomnan (c628-704) twice visited Northumbria probably in 686 and 688 as an ambassador of the Irish sent to re-establish friendly relations with Northumbria under Aldfrith. He was the ninth abbot of Iona and it was while holding that office that he wrote the *Life of Columba* sometime after his second visit to Northumbria. Iona's influence had waned by Bede's day as a result of the refusal to adopt Roman ways. In 686 he took sixty prisoners taken by Ecgfrith in 684 back to Ireland. During his second visit in 688 he visited Wearmouth-Jarrow and discussed the differences between the Roman and Irish churches. He accepted the Roman Easter and tonsure but was unsuccessful in his attempt to persuade the Iona community to adopt them. He went in about 692 with some sympathetic monks from Iona to northern Ireland where monks not under the influence of Iona had adopted Roman ways. When Adomnan was abbot Arculf a bishop from Gaul visited Iona. Arculf had travelled in the eastern Mediterranean and the information he provided was set down by Adomnan in the book *On the Holy Places*. The book contains the earliest known written account of Saint George and it is significant that Saint Paul's church at Jarrow was dedicated on Saint George's day.

Later, about 710, Jarrow was subject to another representation, this time a delegation, probably priests, from Nechtan IV whom Bede describes as king of "all the provinces of the Picts" for discussion on the disputed issues of Easter and the tonsure. Nechtan also asked for architects to build him a stone church in the Roman style. The visit may have provided one occasion on which Bede received information about Nynia. As well as sending architects Ceolfrith provided a refutation prepared in whole or in part by Bede and copied into the *Ecclesiastical History* of the arguments of those still in favour of the Irish Easter. In written form the letter provided increased authority for Nechtan when he changed to Roman practices and destroyed the old Easter tables. Monks in his territory (which included Iona) refusing to accept the changes were expelled in 717 (Iona had conformed the year before). Nechtan himself entered a monastery in 724.

On 12 May 688 Ceolfrith was appointed sole abbot of the two monasteries because of the ill-health of both Biscop and Sigfrith. Sigfrith died of a lung disease on 22 August and Biscop on 12 January 689. Biscop's last wishes were that his library should be kept intact and that both houses should be ruled by an abbot who would not succeed as of hereditary right but was to be elected on grounds of ability. This contrasts with Wilfrid's nomination of a relative to succeed him at Ripon and the succession at Whitby within the kingdom's ruling family. Ceolfrith ruled Wearmouth-Jarrow for slightly more than twenty-eight years. In 716 there were some six hundred monks and the combined estates comprised nearly 150 hides of land. Ecgfrith's endowment was of 110 hides. Just before Biscop died he was arranging the exchange of 8 hides near the (unidentifiable) river Fresca from Aldfrith for a book on cosmography which Biscop had brought from Rome. This estate was later exchanged with a cash payment for a larger one of 28 hides at another unidentifiable place Sambuce during Osred's reign. A further estate of 10 hides possibly at Dalton-le-Dale was bought by a man named Witmær who joined Wearmouth. Under Biscop and Ceolfrith Wearmouth-Jarrow enjoyed links with Rome and Gaul as well as Irish and Pictish foundations especially those which were centres of learning not to mention other Northumbrian monasteries. A group of monks which included Hwætberht were known to have been in Rome in 701 when Sergius was pope and brought back a letter of privilege similar to that secured by Biscop which was confirmed by a synod in the presence of Aldfrith.

At the age of 74 Ceolfrith in failing health left Jarrow for Rome on the morning of Thursday 4 June 716 after mass had been celebrated in the two churches at Wearmouth and a farewell speech given at the oratory of Saint Lawrence. The journey had been planned but Bede who had been influenced more by Ceolfrith than Biscop in a letter to Acca felt the departure as sudden and unexpected. His successor Hwætberht (born about 680) was elected by the brothers of both houses on Whit Sunday in Saint Peter's Wearmouth. He was known as Eusebius because of his piety. It was under this name that he wrote a collection of Latin riddles. Bede dedicated two of his works to him. Hwætberht wrote a letter of commendation to Pope Gregory II for Ceolfrith and gave it to Ceolfrith catching him up at Ælfberht's monastery (taken to be the cell founded by Wilgisl) near the mouth of the Humber. Hwætberht was then confirmed as abbot by Acca, bishop of Hexham. Ceolfrith set sail on Saturday 4 July. He arrived in France on 12 August, was received by King Chilperic II who gave him letters of passage through his kingdom and proceeded to Langres in Burgundy on 25 September. He died the same day at 4.00 pm. He was buried at Langres although Alcuin says that his remains were brought to Wearmouth at a later date. Some monks returned home while others carried on taking with them the *Codex Amiatinus* which Ceolfrith intended for Rome. The *Codex* was one of three pandects or complete copies of the Bible produced by several scribes under Ceolfrith's personal direction at Wearmouth-Jarrow. It is now in Florence but it was possessed by the monastery of Monte Amiate seventy miles from Rome and after which it was named. All that survives of the other two pandects amounts to ten leaves used in Nottinghamshire to provide covers for chartuleries drawn up in the early sixteenth century and one leaf which had been used as the cover of an accounts book in about 1780 and discovered in a bookshop in Newcastle upon Tyne in 1889. Hwætberht's letter was received by Gregory and his reply is to be found in the *Life of Ceolfrith*.

Epilogue

BEDE DIED ON WEDNESDAY 25 MAY 735 AT JARROW. A moving eyewitness account of his last days is given in a letter by a monk of Jarrow called Cuthbert to a colleague Cuthwine. Cuthbert was a pupil of Bede's, possibly a favourite, who later became its abbot. He tells how just before Easter Bede was troubled by weakness and had much difficulty breathing although he felt little pain. From then until Ascension Day remaining cheerful he continued to teach, sing psalms and meditate. He also worked on a translation into the vernacular of Saint John's Gospel as well as some extracts from the works of Isidore of Seville. On the (Tues)day before Ascension Day (the twenty-fourth) his breathing problems increased and his feet began to swell. The following day aware of his approaching end he dictated the concluding chapter of his translation to a boy named Wilberht and distributed his few effects: pepper, linen and incense. He asked the priests of the monastery to offer masses and prayers for him. In the evening Wilberht took down one last sentence and turned him to face the place where he prayed in his cell. After chanting "Glory be to the Father, and to the Son, and to the Holy Spirit" to its end Bede passed away.

Bede as scholar had no equal in his day. He regarded the period covered by the *Ecclesiastical History* as a golden age. Alcuin the only other well-known Northumbrian scholar viewed that part of his own lifetime in which Egbert was first archbishop of York and Saint Peter's School took over from Wearmouth-Jarrow as a centre of learning in similar terms. Yet it was the seventh century which produced such distinctive figures as Cuthbert, Hild, Wilfrid and John.

The written sources for Bede's Northumbria are limited and mostly take the form of hagiography and homily. As a result of their preoccupation with religious matters there is an imbalance in the picture they provide of the seventh and early eighth centuries. Religious concerns must be set in a wider social context, one in which kings struggled for survival and ordinary people got on with the precarious business of living their daily lives. Moreover the

101

prominence given to the *Ecclesiastical History* together with the accounts of Cuthbert and Wilfrid and lack of comparable materials for later periods has tended to somewhat obscure for many the fact that Northumbria did not disappear from the historical scene but as a kingdom survived until the tenth century. But when people think of Anglo-Saxon Northumbria they think of Bede's Northumbria. This can only serve to emphasise that, the issues for the historian apart, what is relevant for people today about Bede's golden age is that in it lie the roots of their Christianity and sense of regional identity.

Table: Framework of Northumbrian chronology

KINGS	SECULAR	BISHOPS	CHURCH
547 IDA			
593 ÆTHELFRITH	535 Edwin born		
	603 *Degsastan*		
	604 Oswald born		
	605 *Chester*		
	612 Oswiu born		
	614 Hild born		
616 EDWIN	616 *Idle*		
	619 Edwin married Æthelburh		
		625 PAULINUS	
	626 Eanflæd born Edwin fought West Saxons		
			627 Edwin, Hild baptized
			628 Biscop born

103

KINGS	SECULAR	BISHOPS	CHURCH
633 **EANFRITH** (Bernicia) **OSRIC** (Deira)	633 *Meicen* *Hatfield Chase*		
634 **OSWALD**	634 *Denisesburn*		634 Cuthbert and Wilfrid born
		635 AIDAN	c640 Hartlepool founded
642 **OSWIU**	642 *Maserfelth* Oswiu married Eanflæd Oswine, sub-king of Deira		642 Ceolfrith born
			644 Paulinus died
	645 Ecgfrith born		
	647 Æthelburh died		648 Hild recalled by Aidan
			650 Eosterwine born
	651 Oswine murdered Æthelwold, sub-king of Deira	651 FINAN	

653	Cedd in Mercia / Wilfrid and Biscop left for Rome (Biscop's 1st visit to Rome)		
654	Cedd bishop of East Saxons		654 Ælfflæd born
655			*Winwæd*
657	Whitby founded		
658	Willibrord born		
c660	Ripon vacated by Eata and given to Wilfrid		
661		COLMAN	
664	Synod of Whitby / Cedd died	TUDA / WILFRID / CHAD	c664 Alhfrith rebelled
664-8	Biscop's 2nd and 3rd visits to Rome		
669	Chad bishop of Mercia	WILFRID	
c669	Eddius came to Northumbria		

KINGS	SECULAR	BISHOPS	CHURCH
670 ECGFRITH	c670 Ælfwine sub-king of Deira	677 BOSA (York) EATA (Hexham/Lindisfarne) EADHÆD (Lindsey)	671 Biscop's 4th journey to Rome
			672 Chad died / Synod of Hertford
			c672-3 Wilfrid granted Hexham / Æthelthryth went to Coldingham / Bede born
			673-4 Wearmouth founded
			c675 Colman died
			676 Cuthbert on Farne
			677 Wilfrid left for Rome
			677-8 Wilfrid in Frisia
			c678 Biscop's 5th visit to Rome

		Trent
679	Wilfrid's appeal heard at Rome Eadhæd expelled from Lindsey		679	*Trent*
680	Wilfrid imprisoned Cædmon died Hild died			
c680	Hwætberht born			
681	Wilfrid in exile Jarrow monastery founded Ceolfrith abbot Eosterwine abbot of Wearmouth	681	TUNBERHT (Hexham) TRUMWINE (Abercorn) EADHÆD (Ripon)		
			c683	Æbbe died
684	Biscop's 6th (last) visit to Rome Tunberht expelled from Hexham		684	Berht's Irish campaign

KINGS	SECULAR	BISHOPS		CHURCH	
685 ALDFRITH	685 *Nechtansmere*	685	CUTHBERT (Hexham, Lindisfarne) EATA (Hexham)	685	Jarrow church dedicated Trumwine vacated Abercorn
	686 Adomnan's first visit to Northumbria	686	WILFRID (Hexham)	686	Eata died Eosterwine died Sigfrith abbot of Wearmouth
		687	JOHN (Hexham) WILFRID (Ripon) EADBERHT (Lindisfarne)	687	Cuthbert died Wilfrid administered Lindisfarne
				688	Ceolfrith abbot of Wearmouth-Jarrow Sigfrith died Adomnan's 2nd visit to Northumbria
				689	Biscop died
				690	Willibrord in Frisia
				691	Second expulsion of Wilfrid
				693	Swithberht consecrated

Year	Event	Year	Bishop	Year	Event	Year	King
695	Willibrord consecrated archbishop			697	Osthryth murdered		
698	Cuthbert's remains elevated	698	EADFRITH (Lindisfarne)	698	Berht killed in Pictish campaign		
c698	*Lindisfarne Gospels* written						
c700	Echternach monastery founded						
702	Synod at Austerfield Wilfrid visited Willibrord						
704	Wilfrid's last appeal heard at Rome						
705	Bosa died			705	Aldfrith died Eadwulf took the throne		
706	Synod at Nidd	706	JOHN (York) WILFRID (Hexham)			**706**	**OSRED**

KINGS	SECULAR	BISHOPS	CHURCH
		709 ACCA (Hexham)	709 Wilfrid died
716 COENRED	711 Picts defeated by Berhtfrith		713 Swithberht died
	c713-4 Ælfflæd died		716 Hwætberht abbot of Wearmouth-Jarrow; Ceolfrith died
718 OSRIC		718 WILFRID II (York)	718 John retired
		721 ÆTHELWOLD (Lindisfarne)	721 John died
729 CEOLWULF -757		c730 PECTHELM (Whithorn)	729 Egbert died
			731 *Ecclesiastical History* completed
737 Eadberht (EIDBIERHT)	RUNIC INSCRIPTION BIRKLEY FONT	732 FRITHUBERHT (Hexham) EGBERT (York)	732 Acca deposed Wilfrid II retired
			734 Frithuberht consecrated
758 SECEDED + RETIRED TO YORK - BRITHER735		735 EGBERT first archbishop of York	735 Bede died

Select Bibliography

Original sources

Most of the written sources are given below. They are listed under editor or translator. Modern English translations are provided in full except where marked with an asterisk.

Allott S	*Alcuin of York — His Life and Letters* (1974)
Anderson A O	*Early Sources of Scottish History AD 500 to 1286* (Volume One) (1922, 1990)
Anderson A O and M O	*Adomnan's Life of Columba* (1961)
Boutflower D S	*Anonymous Life of Ceolfrith* (1912, 1991)
Colgrave B	*The Life of Bishop Wilfrid by Eddius Stephanus* (1927)
	Two Lives of St. Cuthbert (1940)
	The Earliest Life of Gregory the Great (1968)
Colgrave B and Mynors R A B	*Bede's Ecclesiastical History of the English People* (1969)
Emerton E	*The Letters of Saint Boniface* (1940)
Garmonsway G N	*The Anglo-Saxon Chronicle* (2nd edn. 1954)
Godman P	*Alcuin: The Bishops, Kings and Saints of York* (1983)
Haddan A W and Stubbs W	*Councils and Ecclesiastical Documents Relating to Great Britain and Ireland (Volume 3)*★ (1871)
Hood A B E	*St. Patrick. His writings and Muirchu's Life* (1978)
Jackson K H	*The Gododdin. The Oldest Scottish Poem* (1969)
Morris J R	*Nennius' British History and the Welsh Annals* (1980)
Plummer C	*The Historical Works of Bede*★ (1896)
Raine J	*The Priory of Hexham*★ (1863)
	The Historians of the Church of York and its Archbishops★ (1879)
Sherley-Price L (rev. Latham R E)	*Bede: A History of the English Church and People* (1968)

Skene W F	*Chronicles of the Picts and Scots** (1867)
Stephenson J	*Symeon of Durham: A History of the Kings of England* (1858, 1987)
	Symeon of Durham: A History of the Church of Durham (1988)
Sweet H	*The Oldest English Texts** (1885)
Talbot C H	*The Anglo-Saxon Missionaries in Germany* (1954)
Whitelock D	*English Historical Documents Volume One c500-1042* (1955)
Whitelock D (with Douglas D C and Tucker S I)	*The Anglo-Saxon Chronicle: A Revised Translation* (1961)
Wilcock P	*The Lives of the Abbots of Wearmouth* (1818, 1973)
Williams I and J E C	*The Poems of Taliesin** (1968)
Winterbottom M	*Gildas: The Ruin of Britain* (1979)

Selected Modern Works

Only those works most relevant to early Northumbria are listed here. Ideas for wider reading can be found in their bibliographies and a number of national and local periodicals. The publications of the Council for British Archaeology, the *English Historical Review*, and *Anglo-Saxon England* are particularly useful. A number of articles have been reprinted in some of the collections in this bibliography. *The Jarrow Lectures* are also well worth consulting.

Alcock L A	*Arthur's Britain. History and Archaeology AD 367-634* (1971)
Backhouse J	*The Lindisfarne Gospels* (1981)
Baker D ed.	*Medieval Women* (1978)
Barley M W and Hanson R P C eds.	*Christianity in Britain 300-700* (1968)
Bassett S ed.	*The Origins of Anglo-Saxon Kingdoms* (1989)
Battiscombe C F	*The Relics of Saint Cuthbert* (1956)
Blair P H	*Introduction to Anglo-Saxon England* (1956)
	Roman Britain and Early England 55 BC - AD 871 (1963)
	The World of Bede (1970, 1990)
	Northumbria in the Days of Bede (1976)
	Anglo-Saxon Northumbria (1984)
Bonner G ed.	*Famulus Christi: Studies in Commemoration of the Thirteenth Centenary of the birth of the Venerable Bede* (1976)

Bonner G, Rollason D, Stancliffe C eds.	*St. Cuthbert. His Cult and His Community to AD 1200* (1989)
Cameron K	*English Place-names* (3rd edn, 1977)
Campbell J ed.	*The Anglo-Saxons* (1982)
Campbell J	*Essays in Anglo-Saxon History* (1986)
Chadwick N K ed.	*Studies in Early British History* (1954)
	Celt and Saxon: Studies in the Early British Border (1963)
Clemoes P and Hughes K eds.	*England before the Conquest* (1971)
Ekwall E	*The Concise Oxford Dictionary of English Place-Names* (4th edn, 1960)
Godfrey C J	*The Church in Anglo-Saxon England* (1962)
Harrison K	*The Framework of Anglo-Saxon History to AD 900* (1976)
Higham N	*The Northern Counties to AD 1000* (1986)
Hill D	*An Atlas of Anglo-Saxon England* (1981)
Hope-Taylor B	*Under York Minster: Archaeological Discoveries 1966-71* (1971)
	Yeavering. An Anglo-British Centre of Early Northumbria (1977)
Kirby D P ed.	*Saint Wilfrid at Hexham* (1974)
Knowles D	*Saints and Scholars* (1962)
Lapidge M and Gneuss H eds.	*Learning and Literature in Anglo-Saxon England* (1985)
Levison W	*England and the Continent in the Eighth Century* (1946)
Mayr-Harting H	*The Coming of Christianity to Anglo-Saxon England* (1972, 1991)
Morris J R	*The Age of Arthur: A History of the British Isles from 350 to 650* (1973)
Myres J N L	*The English Settlements* (1986)
Rahtz P, Dickinson P and Watts L eds.	*Anglo-Saxon Cemeteries* (1980)
Rollason D	*Saints and Relics in Anglo-Saxon England* (1989)
Sawyer P H	*From Roman Britain to Norman England* (1978)
Stenton F M	*Preparatory to Anglo-Saxon England* (1970)
	Anglo-Saxon England (3rd edn, 1971)
Thomas C	*Christianity in Roman Britain to AD 500* (1981)
	Celtic Britain (1986)
Thompson A H ed.	*Bede, His Life, Times and Writings* (1935)

Wallace-Hadrill J M   *Bede's Ecclesiastical History of the English People:*
                         A Historical Commentary (1988)

Ward B   *The Venerable Bede* (1991)

Wilson D M ed.   *The Archaeology of Anglo-Saxon England* (1976)

Wormald P, Bullough D,   *Ideal and Reality in Frankish and Anglo-Saxon Society*
Collins R eds.   (1983)

Yorke B   *Kings and Kingdoms of Early Anglo-Saxon England* (1990)

Two books, not in themselves sources being part-fiction, but which are
helpful in depicting the age are Anne Warin *Hilda: An Anglo-Saxon Chronicle*
(1989) and *Wilfrid: AD 634 to 709* (1992).